Feng shui
your kitchen

Feng shui
your kitchen

Sharon Stasney

Sterling Publishing Co., Inc. New York
A Sterling/Chapelle Book

Chapelle, Ltd.:

- Owner: Jo Packham
- Editor: Laura Best
- Photography: Scot Zimmerman, Scot Zimmerman Photography
  Kevin Dilley, Hazen Photography
- Illustrations: Shauna Mooney Kawasaki
- Staff: Areta Bingham, Kass Burchett, Ray Cornia, Jill Dahlberg, Marilyn Goff, Karla Haberstitch, Holly Hollingsworth, Susan Jorgensen, Barbara Milburn, Karmen Quinney, Caroll Shreeve, Cindy Stoeckl, Kim Taylor, Sara Toliver, Desirée Wybrow

If you have any questions or comments, please contact:
Chapelle, Ltd., Inc., P.O. Box 9252, Ogden, UT 84409
(801) 621-2777 • (801) 621-2788 Fax
e-mail: chapelle@chapelleltd.com
web site: chapelleltd.com

Library of Congress Cataloging-in-Publication Data Available

The written instructions, photographs, illustrations, and artwork in this volume are intended for the personal use of the reader and may be reproduced for that purpose only. Any other use, especially commercial use, is forbidden under law without the written permission of the copyright holder. Every effort has been made to ensure that all information in this book is accurate. However, due to differing conditions, tools, and individual skills, the publisher cannot be responsible for any injuries, losses, and/or other damages which may result from the use of information in this book.

This volume is meant to stimulate decorating ideas. If readers are unfamiliar or not proficient in a skill necessary to attempt a project, we urge them to refer to an instructional book specifically addressing the technique required.

10 9 8 7 6 5 4 3 2

Published by Sterling Publishing Co., Inc.
387 Park Avenue South, New York, NY 10016
©2002 by Sharon Stasney
Distributed in Canada by Sterling Publishing
c/o Canadian Manda Group, 165 Dufferin Street
Toronto, Ontario, Canada M6K 3H6
Distributed in Great Britain by Chrysalis Books Group PLC
The Chrysalis Building, Bramley Road, London W10 6SP, England
Distributed in Australia by Capricorn Link (Australia) Pty. Ltd.
P.O. Box 704, Windsor, NSW 2756, Australia

Printed in China
All Rights Reserved

Sterling ISBN 0-8069-7383-8

Introduction to feng shui

This book invites you to look at your kitchen in a completely different way than you have before. Although you probably found this book in the interior design section of the bookstore, it's actually about life design. Using the principles and teachings of an ancient art called feng shui, this book will help you understand how your kitchen is a microcosm of your entire life. Your personality, patterns, relationships, and struggles are all figuratively there, in your kitchen.

Coming from the Chinese culture, feng shui focuses on how humans interact with their environment. At its most basic level, it provides a language for understanding how environments mirror the people that live in them. It also provides a complete system that humans can use to influence their environments. Using feng shui, we can create environments that put into place the patterns and life situations we would like to enjoy. Once those are in place in our environment, it is much easier to create them in our lives.

Our blood is sea water: it remembers tides, the moon's pull. In the hollow of the womb in each of us is life evolving from the sea.

Nancy Newhall
This is the American Earth

Table of contents

Feng shui concepts

Chi

8

Chi is the life force that animates or brings something to life. The more chi something has, the more powerful its life force and presence. Weak chi in the body can manifest as apathy, fatigue, lack of appetite, depression, coldness, and susceptibility to disease. In life, weak chi can manifest as a lack of opportunities, narrow or limited thinking, the inability to make decisions, or constant setbacks. To improve your life situation, gather and strengthen your chi.

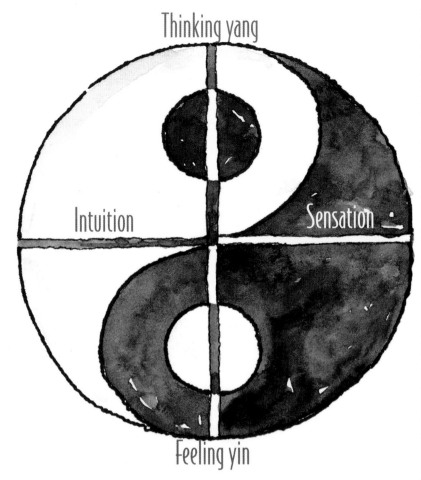

Thinking yang

Intuition

Sensation

Feeling yin

We are constantly in a cycle of energy moving from still to active, thoughts to feelings, up to down, and out to in.

Yin & yang

Yin and yang are two ends of a continuum that describe how energy (chi) moves. The yin aspect moves chi inward, slowing it down and cooling it off. Therefore, any décor choice that slows the movement of chi, makes you feel introspective, or cools a room, is a yin item. Yang is the opposite force. It speeds up chi, spirals it outward, and increases heat. Any décor choice that brings in more light (heat generator), more colors (activity), more movement, more patterns, or other forms of stimuli, increases yang.

If you want your kitchen to get you going in the morning, encourage you to cook, encourage you to eat, or help you feel motivated, lean toward the yang side of the spectrum.

If you want your kitchen to feel restful, relaxing, and peaceful—a quiet place you retreat to at the end of the day, include yin choices.

Using intention

Using intention means to consciously decide what you want in life and then set out to create it. This is not something you instinctively know how to do. It requires the ability to direct your focus in a particular way. Decide on something you would like to change in your life and write it down.

Describe your intention. Think what you want, not what you don't want; and be specific.

Don't tell the universe how to create it for you. If you leave the means open, the universe can be more creative than you could ever imagine in finding ways to realize your intention.

Change your focus from wanting to having. A powerful shift in energy occurs when your mental state changes from wishing something would happen, to expecting it to happen, to acting as if it has already happened. This positive thinking frees your psychic energy to begin interacting with the world in the way you would if you had already achieved your desired goal.

10

Ways to increase yin

Lighting
- Install a dimmer switch on lights.

Colors
- Consider dark floor colors and wood finishes.

- Use a neutral color scheme.

Density & space
- Add more furnishings.

- Replace lightweight pieces with more substantial ones.

- Replace plastic pots with heavy terra-cotta pots.

- Fill open spaces with plants, baskets, or pots.

- Pad the chairs.

- Add a throw or a pillow.

- Replace dining chairs with a built-in bench.

Shapes
- Use soft, rounded shapes.

Windows & floor
- Add a pull shade to windows to cut glare.

- Replace mini blinds with hanging drapes.

- Add large rugs to hardwood or tile floors.

Ways to increase yang

Lighting
- **Add more lighting.**

Colors
- **Use white or bright colors.**

- **Use high-gloss paint on trim.**

- **Display a multicolored painting or one full of activity.**

- **Add a bright-colored teakettle.**

Density & space
- **Widen doorways.**

- **Remove unnecessary furniture.**

- **Clear off counters and streamline appliances.**

Shapes
- **Replace hanging plants with plants that extend upward.**

- **Use strong shapes such as triangles, straight lines, upward pillars, etc.**

Windows & floor
- **Keep floors bare.**

- **Replace hanging drapes with blinds.**

- **Hang bright, light-reflective objects in windows.**

- **Add a skylight.**

Weak & strong kitchens

In traditional feng shui, there were two sets of rules used to judge a home's suitability to sustain positive chi. These were called the weak (hsu) five and the strong (shi) five. A specialized subset of these rules pertain specifically to the kitchen. If you're uncertain of where to start, you can't go wrong working to rid yourself of hsu and add more shi to your kitchen.

A careful look at this kitchen reveals numerous "chi generating" features. Signs of life include fresh flowers, family activities posted on the fridge, a parrot on patrol, streaming sunlight, and living plants. A thriving environment nourishes the spirit just as food nourishes the physical body.

A large kitchen needs live bodies to energetically "fill it." This kitchen is home to ten active children, but on those days when there are not many people around, small touches can help keep energy moving:

☯ **canopy lighting**

☯ **sunlight**

☯ **fresh flowers**

☯ **cooking oils and utensils**

The weak five (hsu)

Some conditions in the kitchen repel or dilute chi. The following five weaknesses should be avoided in a kitchen:

A large kitchen that does not get much use. A large kitchen needs a large family and a love of entertaining. Avoid the palatial show kitchen, with granite countertops and marble floors, that lacks liveliness. From a feng shui perspective, a large kitchen with few people places too much stress on the few to generate the energy necessary to keep such a large space active. Inactive dormant chi in a kitchen weakens the occupant's life force.

A stove that's never used. Since the stove's job is transforming raw nutrients into nurturing meals, an inactive stove represents the occupant's inability to transform opportunities (potential chi) into actual manifestations (kinetic chi). If you find yourself in this position, boil water on the burners, even if you don't cook.

To increase feelings of safety, encase knives in a wooden block and add under-cabinet lighting to soften (melt) any remaining sharpness.

Dangerous items in the kitchen. The kitchen houses the greatest risk to physical safety by containing fire, knives, and slippery surfaces. Your design and décor choices should minimize risk and increase a feeling of safety. Keep knives away from the stove; these two items together represent the greatest potential injury.

An open kitchen with too many doorways. Modern kitchens are completely open to the rest of the house. Although this open design is acceptable, if there is nothing holding energy in and allowing it to pool and rest, reserves are quickly depleted. The ability to hold energy in reserve is a Water quality, and Water needs Earth to contain its essence. Balance out too many doorways by bringing in large earthen pots and other containers to give the energy a place to gather.

Neglect manifests as uncleanliness. Clutter and uncleanliness represent energy that has advanced beyond the ripe stage to the rotting, deteriorating stage. Just as rotting fruit attracts flies, dirty cluttered kitchens attract death and decay. The only remedy for this is cleaning and decluttering. Get the help you need (professional organizers, a cleaning service) to make this an actuality in your life.

Where do I start?

Feng shui can be intimidating and overwhelming. Start any feng shui analysis by making three lists:

- **things you love about your home, just as it is**

- **things you dislike and want to change**

- **things you want in your home but don't have**

These three lists are your key to discovering your likes, dislikes, and desires in life. Your external environment is a mirror of your internal reality.

The first list represents the aspects of yourself that you have owned and integrated into your personality. The second list represents your "shadow" traits, parts or yourself that you hide and resist. The third list represents your potential, traits that you project onto others (or other people's homes) because you haven't yet found a way to manifest them in your own life.

Too much white in a kitchen makes it feel sterile and unwelcoming. Simply adding fresh fruit, flowers, or green plants can bring an otherwise dead room to life.

Look for signs of life. Animals, thriving green plants, and children running around, all attract healthy positive chi. Have as many plants, pets, and children around as you can take good care of and keep clean. Some people have so many pets around that they lose their ability to keep things smelling and looking clean. Others create such a sterile environment that even a plastic plant would wilt. Find your happy medium.

The strong five (shi)

Just as conditions repel or dilute chi, other conditions attract and strengthen it. The following five strengths should serve as the basis for your kitchen planning, regardless of personal preferences.

Keep fresh food visible and accessible. By placing food (potential nourishment) within our view, we associate the kitchen with a place that has the ability to nurture us. Our subconscious gets the message that there is plenty and that our needs will be taken care of. Our beliefs about food form the core of our beliefs about money. To have enough of one is to have enough of the other.

Design a kitchen that gets used. Just as your body requires exercise to stay strong, your kitchen needs regular use to keep the chi associated with physical well-being active and positive. If you don't cook, be certain to bring other elements into your kitchen that you do use. You might place a piano in this space or a reading chair with books. Make the kitchen a room you enjoy.

Invite life into your kitchen. Whether you have a child, a pet, or a plant, living entities will bring positive chi into a room.

Keep it clean. The ancient Chinese believed that dirty, unkempt spaces encouraged dark and evil spirits into a home, who brought with them illness and disease. A more modern reading is that dirt and clutter cause chi to stagnate, weakening the immune system and inhibiting its ability to move pollutants and toxins through the body quickly. The stove is the most important area of all. Be certain it's clean after each meal.

Take care of your water supply. Clean water is the basis of human life. Take pains to improve the quality of the water you drink. Don't allow faucets to run while doing dishes and get dripping faucets fixed. If you diminish your own precious resources through apathy and neglect, why should the universe entrust more resources to you?

Food for thought: If you were going to make an offering to the earth in thanks for the abundance in your life, what would your offering look like?

Zao Wang Ye

To facilitate the harmony between heaven, earth, and humanity, the Chinese believed in a god who communicated between heaven and humans regarding the kitchen. The god's name was Zao Wang Ye, and his job was to make annual reports to heaven as to whether or not the humans living in the house were obeying divine law. If a household was obedient, Zao Wang Ye promised to bring abundance and ensure that there was enough to eat (food was scarce in China and abundance was often equated with having enough food). If heaven's laws were not obeyed, the inhabitants could not be assured that they would have food to eat, and they would need to pay a penance to regain favor.

Many feng shui rituals surrounding stoves and kitchens can be traced back to this ancient god's likes and dislikes. However, modern societies would do well to remember that all cultures must eat to survive. Therefore, food, and the environment in which we prepare and eat it, is the strongest universal abundance symbol there is.

The ba gua

Many cultures associate a home with the cycle of life. The Chinese call this concept the ba gua, literally translated as "eight sectors."

The ba gua is a template, or map, that describes how chi moves from one aspect of your life to another to create a life cycle. According to the ba gua, each area or sector of your physical environment is associated with a certain life aspect. Each sector has an energy pattern and symbols that will strengthen the life aspect associated with that area.

The ba gua map represents a balanced flow of energy through all cycles of life. This refrigerator version of a ba gua map reminds the residents that life is a cycle and each phase in the cycle deserves attention.

Abundance—Running horses display one grasping opportunities, rather than letting them pass by.

Family—Pictures of parents and ancestors can bring the energy of these people into our daily lives.

Self-knowledge—Mountains reflect the need for a strong sense of self and personal boundaries.

External Recognition—A Zen card displays the Transformation figure.

Health—This exuberant figure brings vivacious and healthy chi to the center of this ba gua cycle.

New Beginnings—Literally called "Chaos" in the I Ching, this sector stands for limitless potential. Any symbol of death, rebirth, chaos, or water is appropriate.

Intimate Relationships—Personal notes and the image of a couple honor commitment and marriage.

Creativity—Photos of children or creative projects remind you to play and embrace the child inside.

Helpful People—A chime rings when the freezer door opens, activating spirit guides and angels as a reminder that you are not alone.

Ba gua–the cycle of life

The ba gua is a map that reveals the mystical connections between energy patterns in your physical environment and what's happening in different areas of your life. Identifying where each life area is in your home provides valuable insight into what adjustments you'll want to make to create what you want both in your home and in your life.

The ba gua is traditionally drawn as an octagon. This eight-sided shape was the combination of a circle (dynamic yang force) and a square (stabilizing yin force).

The above circle depicts each area of the ba gua as part of the cycle of life.

How you decorate the areas of your home and the kitchen will affect those aspects of your life. The ba gua is rich in symbolism and a bit tricky to work with in the home.

REAR LEFT ABUNDANCE	REAR CENTER EXTERNAL RECOGNITION	REAR RIGHT INTIMATE RELATIONSHIPS
MIDDLE LEFT FAMILY & ANCESTORS	MIDDLE CENTER HEALTH	MIDDLE RIGHT CREATIVITY & CHILDREN
FRONT LEFT SELF KNOWLEDGE	FRONT CENTER NEW BEGINNINGS	FRONT RIGHT HELPFUL PEOPLE

ENTRANCE GRID — MOUTH OF CHI

The entrance grid orients you to the different sectors and their relative placement in your home. Use the information in the following chapter along with this map in designing and decorating your home.

New Beginnings

The ba gua begins in the New Beginnings sector. Each lifetime is a new journey, but so is each day, each relationship, and each life phase. Graduation from college signifies a New Beginning, so does life as a married person or as a divorced person. They all require the emergence of a new identity, sometimes a new name, and new responsibilities and opportunities for growth. This emergence from a womb or neutral beginning point is marked by the color black, representing the union of all, and the element Water, the depths from which each new beginning arises. Flowing forms and shapes are related to this area because they create the downward-moving, flowing energy associated with Water.

The turtle is a New Beginnings symbol, because he carries everything with him that he needs for his journey, signifying that we each have all that we need to make each new beginning successful. Turtles also represent the creative force and the union of heaven (turtle's upper shell) with the earth (turtle's body and underbelly), the force that activates and gets the birthing process going.

Anytime you begin a new life path such as a new job, new relationship, or new home, activate the New Beginnings area of the ba gua.

Single items such as this chair represent autonomy and independence which are the main goals of the Self-knowledge area.

Self-knowledge

The first stage of development in any new journey is self-discovery, finding out who we are and what we want to accomplish this time around. Newly emerged from the womb, this is a period of learning how to separate, stand on our own, and have well-defined boundaries. Those who develop their own foundation, grounding, and sense of self, are able to reconnect with others further along the cycle, which leads to intimacy and marriage. Those who are unable to separate at this stage find themselves unable to truly give themselves to a partner, since they do not yet have the essential understanding of self that precedes any healthy relating between self and others. This grounding and self-assuredness is represented by the symbol of mountain. The blue color is associated with wisdom, the deepest wisdom being to know the self. Solid heavy shapes and furniture represent a strong sense of self and the ability to stand firm in your own resolve and opinions.

Family & Ancestors

Our development of self begins in childhood. We learn who we are, our skills, our issues, in the incubation tank called our family. The family represents our support structure—those who love and support us while we're growing and learning.

If you find yourself in the position that your family did not or was not able to offer this support, don't feel that you must limit yourself to your biological family. This sector takes in all supportive energies at a time when you feel vulnerable and weak. These are people who teach us new skills and who applaud our first steps. For this reason, the Family area of the ba gua is associated with the trunk of the tree, the forging power. This power is represented by the color green and the spring season, meaning that we are learning and growing at a tremendous rate during this time. In this area, the voices of our ancestors call to us and tell us what is or isn't possible for us. This voice from the past is symbolized by the sound of thunder. All these activities ready us to move out of the home and into the world, so we can give our gifts and share our essence.

Heirlooms and other family symbols represent that we grow best when supported by a loving family.

23

Abundance

The giving of our gifts relates to the Abundance sector of the ba gua, a feeling of energy moving through us and out into the world. More than the accumulation of wealth, Abundance is the ability to give of ourselves. Those who feel truly abundant, have both the means and the desire to give. Money enables us to give, but so do talents, abilities, skills, and time. These gifts generate the same energy as money. Whether our Abundance is money or gifts, the wind, the mover of energy and opportunities, must blow in order to bring blessings. Therefore, this sector encourages us to be flexible and adaptable to whatever our current situation brings.

Abundance is also concerned with preparation for the future. Associated with the spring, this is the time when seeds are planted and buds form on trees, all a signal that we are preparing to reap a future harvest, which comes further along the cycle. We must do the necessary work at this stage in the cycle, to have riches later in life. This sector is related to being active and productive.

Frogs are mythic symbols of prosperity and magic. Typically the frog indicates that the windfall is unexpected and that your life is soon to be transformed.

External Recognition

After working hard to give fully of yourself, it's natural to desire that others recognize and find value in your efforts. This sector is not about being famous, but about being recognized and valued for what you do with your life's energy. We all have a need to feel important and valuable. This sector recognizes that need and encourages us to seek that recognition.

We associate External Recognition or fame with the Fire element, because this sector is concerned with transcending self, becoming more than self, and connecting with others in a way not previously experienced. Here we leave the personal development side of the cycle and enter the realm of interpersonal development. Passion, intensity, and sexual union are all aspects of Fire's heat and ability to consume self. Such heat is associated with summer, noonday, light, and bright colors. Therefore, symbols that represent the transcendence of previously necessary boundaries and the ability to merge with another activate the External Recognition sector of the ba gua.

Roosters are associated with External Recognition because they are fearless in declaring to all the world that they are awake (conscious) and alive.

24

Intimate Relationships

This phase is associated with marriage, which is our society's symbol of the ultimate commitment. If you choose not to marry, mark this phase of your life with a partnership ritual calling forth the same level of commitment and mutual support as marriage. At this phase, we move outside the self and learn to give of ourselves for the benefit of a whole. This commitment might be to mother earth or to a political cause. Regardless of what stirs the energy of commitment in you, your ability to contribute to something outside yourself is essential to progressing further along the life cycle. The Chinese have many symbols of lifelong commitment—carp, the eternal knot, the infinity symbol, and pairs of things. Use items that represent commitment and mutual support to you.

The owners' consciously set their kitchen with two of everything to maintain their commitment to each other.

Creativity & Children

In committed partnerships, creative energy often results in the birth of children. Children represent the individual's ability to extend his or her energy beyond the self. Whether we care for a child, a pet, or a project, we'll feel the joy of Creativity when we extend ourselves in the care of another. This sector also begins the season of reaping, when we pour all that we have learned and become into our children (or creative projects) and see ourselves mirrored in their faces and behavior. Our children remind us to play and be joyful and not take life so seriously. It's time to relax, slow down, and start enjoying the fruits of a lifetime of labor.

The ability to let your fun playful side out of hiding is the essence of the Creativity sector. This hand-painted table turns an ordinary dining room table into a backgammon set.

Create your own mobile of your favorite greeting cards to remind yourself of all the wonderful friends and family in your life. You are not alone.

Health

At the center of the cycling wheel of energy lies the Health sector. The purpose of this sector is to balance and stabilize the individual as he progresses through various stages. If the Health chi is weak, the person feels assaulted, overwhelmed, and confused. Unable to sort and make sense of the new experiences, the body responds by shutting down. Chronic illnesses, frequent fatigue, and other signs of a weakened immune system result.

The best feng shui for this sector is to keep it open and maintain a balanced flow of chi throughout the space. Often referred to as the "spacious hall," chi in the Health area needs to be free to flow from the front of the house to the back and from side to side. Small closed-in closets or stairs are especially difficult to deal with in this area, as the chi moves either too quickly or too slowly.

Helpful People

Keep your Health area as open as possible. This indoor window between the kitchen and dining room opens the space considerably and allows the cook a view of all comings and goings.

Having lived a full rich life, we are in a position to share our wisdom and life experiences to help others. Although this sector is related to the retirement phase of life overall, we are all in a Helpful People stage regarding some aspect of our lives. If you have walked a path before, learned a skill, endured a difficult experience, you are in the Helpful People stage of that experience. Choosing to use your experiences and skills to help and bless others and ease their journey is what makes the chi flow.

In addition to functioning as helpful people, we are also in need of the helpful actions of others. The Helpful People sector reminds us that we do not walk any path alone and that reaching out and connecting with others is part of the journey.

Ba gua characteristics

Element wheel graphic	Colors	Seasons	Time of day	Element	Animal	Shape	Energy pattern
New Beginnings	black		midnight		turtle		
Self-knowledge	blue		dawn				
Family & Ancestry	green		morning		dragon		
Abundance	purple		late morning				
External Recognition	red		noonday		phoenix		
Intimate Relationships	pink		late afternoon				
Creativity & Children	white		evening		tiger		
Helpful People	gray		late evening				
Health	yellow	all seasons	all times		serpent		

REAR LEFT ABUNDANCE	REAR CENTER EXTERNAL RECOGNITION	REAR RIGHT INTIMATE RELATIONSHIPS
MIDDLE LEFT FAMILY & ANCESTORS	MIDDLE CENTER HEALTH	MIDDLE RIGHT CREATIVITY & CHILDREN
FRONT LEFT SELF-KNOWLEDGE	FRONT CENTER NEW BEGINNINGS	FRONT RIGHT HELPFUL PEOPLE

ENTRANCE GRID MOUTH OF CHI

Because the ba gua map represents the cycle of life, each sector influences the surrounding sectors. What happens in one affects the sector directly across on the wheel.

The ba gua helps us see that everything we do in life is interconnected. For example, the ba gua reminds us that our Abundance sector is controlled by our willingness to help others (the Helpful People sector). It also reminds us that we cannot do everything ourselves, and that it is natural to combine forces and call upon others to help. The Intimate Relationship area is anchored to the Self-knowledge area, indicating that healthy balanced relationships can only occur when each individual takes responsibility for who he or she is. This book will help you understand how to plan a remodel or set up your kitchen using the wisdom of the ba gua. Use the diagram on page 28 to orient yourself to the various sectors of the ba gua map and how they are interrelated.

New Beginnings & External Recognition—Getting on the right path is essential to achieving meaningful recognition later in life. If you feel that no one values you or that you aren't receiving the recognition you desire, look to the New Beginnings sector to see if perhaps you need to change your path.

New Beginnings affects External Recognition

Family & Creativity—If you're dealing with difficulties in the Creativity & Children area, often those difficulties originate further back in time. Resolving issues and concerns with your parents can free you to interact with your children in a new and healthier way.

Family affects Creativity

Health—Healthy chi is moving chi. As the balancing agent, the status of your Health sector affects every other ba gua sector. Keep things as open and smooth as possible for optimal health and mental well-being.

Health balances all the sectors

Self-knowledge & Intimate Relationships—No lasting happy relationship can develop unless both individuals know and love first themselves and then each other. Relationship problems can often be resolved by working in the Self-knowledge sector, creating space that helps one or both partners better understand themselves, their needs, and their gifts.

Self-knowledge affects Intimate Relationships

Abundance & Helpful People—Both these sectors are concerned with giving and receiving. If opportunities or money seem scarce, the best way to change it is to give of yourself. Be a helpful person to someone else. Offer your time, or your skills, or your meager supply, and you will feel energized and optimistic. Also, remember that people are ready and available to help you when you need them. Don't hesitate to ask others to serve as mentors or benefactors.

Abundance affects Helpful People

Positioning the ba gua over your kitchen

You can use a separate ba gua just for your kitchen. This map works in concert with the larger house map, just like one system in your body, such as the digestive system, works with the entire body to accomplish its goals. The Chinese teach that the whole is reflected in the parts and vice versa. Each room is a microcosm of energy patterns happening in the entire home. Creating balance and harmony in just one room can ripple out and change the way the entire house feels.

To place the ba gua over your kitchen, identify the main entrance. This might be difficult. Often kitchens have more than one entrance that you use frequently. If this is the case, use the entrance that aligns with the direction of the front door. The wall of the main entrance will be the bottom line of the ba gua map.

When there are more than one entry doors, as represented in the kitchen below, use the door that lines up with the front door.

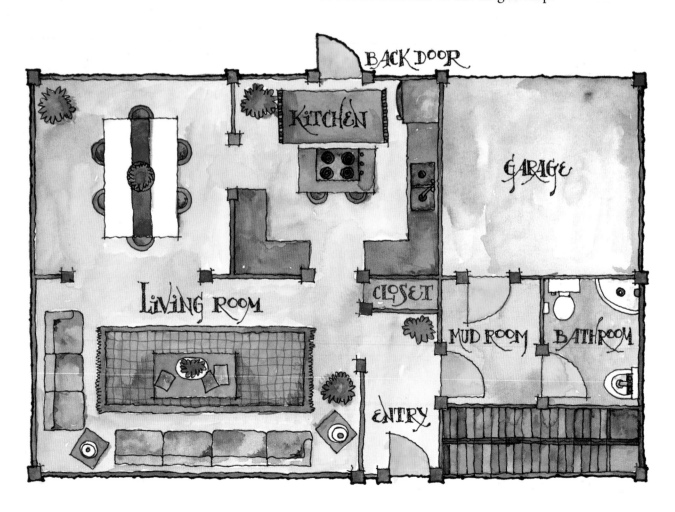

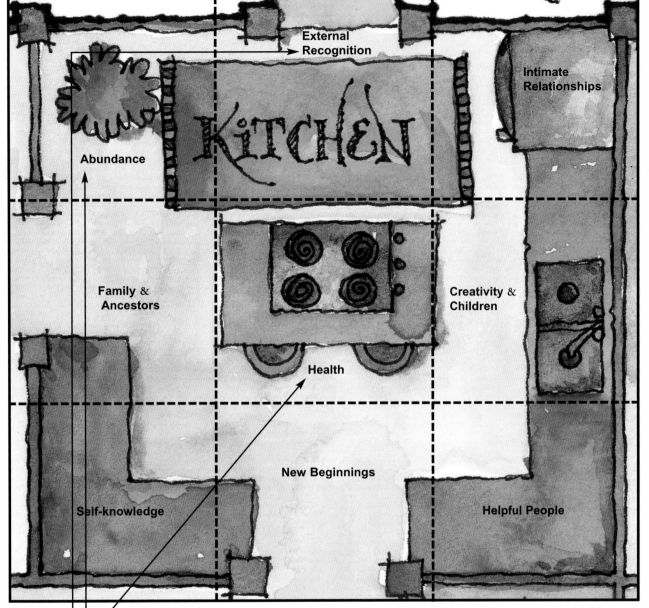

Once you lay the ba gua over a room, you may notice that you have some problems. The floor plan above reveals that the stove falls in the center of the room, placing it in the Health sector. To balance this, be certain you use Wood energy, either tall vertical shapes (tall barstools), the color green (in rugs, countertops, or chair pads, or actual wood (in the island itself.

The Abundance area has a tall green plant, enhancing Wood energy, so no problems there. Intimate Relationships lands on the refrigerator, so be certain to place a picture of you and your sweetie on the refrigerator door.

Notice that the back door is in the External Recognition sector, and the fact that the stove lines up directly with the back door makes for an even stronger External Recognition issue. The owners adjusted for this by placing a red rug horizontally in front of the door. The rug will stop chi from leaving too quickly and generate a stronger Fire vibration in the room.

The five elements

The five energy elements are simply names for the five general ways in which energy converts from one form to another. Stillness and quiet (Water) lead to new growth and activity (Wood), this growth leads to passion, intensity, and fullness (Fire), which ushers in a period of rest and comfort (Earth), which allows time for integration and organizing (Metal), which slows and condenses until energy returns to its dormant stage (back to Water).

The five elements apply to a physical body, the change of seasons, diet choices, furnishings, colors, materials—just about anything can be divided into the five elements. The interesting thing about this system is that the Chinese believe that to shift the elemental cycle in any one of these areas (say, work or home environment) will have an intrinsic, inescapable effect on the balance of the five elements in every other system.

We can use these interrelated changes to make a meaningful difference in our lives. We can change our diets, our décors, or our job choices, which in turn affect our moods, dispositions, and resulting life situations. Every time we create a microcosm of beauty or balance, we increase those forces upon the planet at large, and the chi of the entire world is enhanced.

The basics of the five-element system

Each element is primarily associated with colors, seasons, times of day, parts of the body, emotions, foods, and energy patterns. Increasing or decreasing items associated with each element will strengthen or weaken that element's influence in your home and, therefore, in your life. For example, if you increase bright colors, lots of natural sunlight, and triangular shapes in your home, you are increasing the Fire element. Fire is associated with an active social life, intense feelings, and the ability to transcend boundaries. Increasing Fire items will increase Fire's influence. Therefore, your home will become a more social space, you will tend to feel things more intensely, and you will be able to transcend previous limitations and boundaries.

A personal approach to the elements

- ✆ **Find your primary element.**

- ✆ **Decide whether you need to support or tone down your personal element.**

- ✆ **For support, add more of your element or the element directly before it on the wheel.**

- ✆ **To subdue, add any of the three elements that come after it on the wheel.**

- ✆ **To increase balance, add more of the element before and after your element.**

Water	Wood	Fire	Earth	Metal
Black	Green	Bright color	Brown	Gray
Dark blue	Purple	Star	Muted color	Silver
Wavy	Tall vertical	Triangle	Square	White
Mirror	Living plant	Pyramid	Rectangle	Circle
Glass	Dragon	Starburst	Container	Arc
Water image	Stereo or radio	Candle	Collectible	Organizer
Water in vase	Wind chime	Rooster	Earthenware	Metal item
Hanging plant	Live bamboo	Live animal	Pottery	Metal utensil
Meditation area	Coin	People	Family portrait	Stainless steel
Tea service	Exotic food	Fresh flower	Cushion	Angel
Journal	High placement	Teakettle	Padded chair	Grouping
Turtle	Mobile	Cookware	Throw	Toy
Drape	Frog	Electronic	Antique	Artwork
Fountain	Running horse	Expansive view	Crystal	Craft supply

The grouping in the photograph above contains all five elements. The branches represent Wood. The vase is filled with Water. The candle represents Fire. The circular shapes add Metal. The ceramic candleholder brings in Earth.

Combining elements

Besides understanding each element individually, you also need to understand how the elements affect each other.

Each element has two other elements which enhance or strengthen it and two others that weaken or subdue it. How you combine elements in your space affects the overall impact. Be careful not to get too much or too little of any one element, since balance comes by energy flowing through all five, not just one or two.

The charts on page 35 should help you understand which elements strengthen and which elements weaken or subdue each of the five elements.

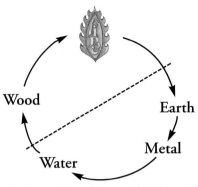

Wood → Earth → Metal → Water (cycle)

To strengthen Fire, add either Fire or Wood. Adding Earth will evolve Fire energy further along the constructive cycle. Adding Metal will drain Fire. Water will subdue it.

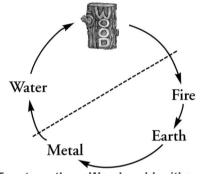

Water → Fire → Earth → Metal (cycle)

To strengthen Wood, add either Wood or Water. Adding Fire will evolve Wood energy further along the constructive cycle. Adding Earth will drain Wood. Metal will subdue it.

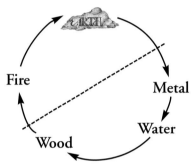

Fire → Metal → Water → Wood (cycle)

To strengthen Earth, add either Earth or Fire energy. Adding Metal will evolve Earth energy further along the constructive cycle. Adding Water will drain Earth. Wood will subdue it.

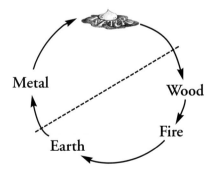

Metal → Wood → Fire → Earth (cycle)

To strengthen Water, add either Water or Metal. Adding Wood will evolve Water energy further along the constructive cycle. Adding Fire will drain Water. Earth will subdue it.

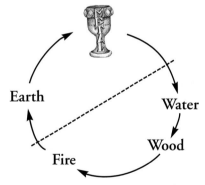

Earth → Water → Wood → Fire (cycle)

To strengthen Metal, add either Metal or Earth. Adding Water will evolve Metal energy further along the constructive cycle. Adding Wood will drain Metal. Fire will subdue it.

Find your type

Designing your kitchen is as influential as choosing your home location. A kitchen, more than any other single room in the house, reveals your core. It indicates what you delight in, how grounded you are in a physical body, whether or not you allow yourself sensual pleasures, and the source of your strength. Different types of kitchens fall into one or more of the five element types. In this book, we'll explore each of these types in detail and show how to create a kitchen that supports your true essence.

Before learning about these five types, take the following five-element questionnaire. Fill out every question in each category. Do not ask others for help. To uncover your essence, you must do your own digging.

Questionnaire scoring

For each question, mark −2 if it is nothing like you, +1 if it is somewhat like you, and +2 if you feel this way often. At the end, add up the score.

36

Type A

❏ I like to get up and get going in the morning.

❏ I love trying new things or doing something that's never been done before.

❏ I am a natural leader and others often look to me to know what to do and when.

❏ I don't always think things through before I start a project. I tend to jump right in and figure it out as I go along.

❏ I don't keep broken or non-functional items. It's easy for me to give things away and clear out clutter.

❏ I feel good when I've accomplished a lot that day. Sitting around watching TV all day would drive me crazy.

❏ I can get frustrated when things don't move at my pace or happen the way I would like them to. I find I often know the best, most efficient way to get things done.

❏ I get bored easily and need to try new things often.

❏ The only way I can slow down throughout the day is to get sick or drop from exhaustion. Otherwise, I just keep on going, doing one thing after the other.

❏ I tend to start new projects before I've finished the old ones. I often have three to four projects going at the same time.

Type B

❏ My house is a gathering place for many people, not just family. I love entertaining. I fear loneliness.

❏ A quiet house makes me feel uncomfortable. I'll turn on a TV or stereo to avoid silence.

❏ I am sometimes captured by the drama of events more than the factual reality. If there is no drama, life feels flat and boring.

❏ I find I'm quite sensitive to other's feelings, even when I don't want to be.

❏ I tend to move quickly from thing to thing. I'll study a little of this and a little of that. Sometimes it's hard for me to focus.

❏ I find I'm easily emotional and have trouble separating my own emotions from others'. I feel it all, and it can get overwhelming.

❏ I live through my senses. Sights, scents, textures, and tastes can transform the ordinary into something wonderful.

❏ I love to laugh and often feel joyous. This rising of emotion can sometimes be followed by a plummeting depression.

❏ I struggle with boundary issues and take on others' causes and opinions quickly.

❏ I'd rather spend money on something beautiful that I use only once a year than something plain that I use every day.

Type C

❑ Home is a place for family to come together.

❑ I like having possessions around me. I'm more interested in comfort than cleanliness.

❑ I tend to keep things just in case someone might need it someday. I want to make certain there's enough for everyone.

❑ I surround myself with photographs. It comforts me to wrap the past around me like a blanket.

❑ Thick walls feel nurturing and supportive. I love the little nooks and crannies of older homes.

❑ I am often the one in charge of organizing events that bring family together, such as reunions and holiday gatherings.

❑ I'd much rather be at home with my kids than socialize with people I don't know very well.

❑ I need to know everyone has what they need, then I can relax. Until then, I can't enjoy myself.

❑ I find I often worry about things that "could" happen or that someone's feelings might be hurt. In fact, it's hard for me to stop worrying, even when I want to.

❑ I like containers. Pots, vases, dressers, buffets, chairs, and couches, all make a room feel more comfortable.

Type D

❑ Cleanliness is my top priority. I can't relax until the floors are swept and mopped. I tend to disinfect things and have an aversion to insects and bugs.

❑ Everything should have a place and stay in place. Things are put away as soon as I'm done using them.

❑ I figure things out in a scientific manner. Results only have meaning if you follow a method that can be tried and tested.

❑ I like a streamlined décor style; too much stuff feels suffocating.

❑ I spend a lot of time in my head and tend to intellectualize things.

❑ I like white because it feels clean and simple. Anything else tends to distract me.

❑ I focus my thoughts easily and am rigorous in my analysis of a problem or event.

❑ I believe in following rules and upholding the law. I fear the chaos that can ensue when people "shoot from the hip" or don't follow procedures.

❑ I like to figure out the best way to do things and then do them that way from that point on. Why waste time and energy doing things in a slow, messy, or inefficient way?

❑ I have a sharp wit and am verbally astute.

Type E

❑ I seek a place of refuge. I want home to be a quiet peaceful place where I can be alone.

❑ Living an honorable life is of primary importance.

❑ I don't notice my surroundings much. I'm often too absorbed in my internal world.

❑ I'm a bit of a night owl and have a hard time waking up early in the morning.

❑ I like to take my time and make certain my choices are in line with my ethics.

❑ I pay more attention to my internal voice than to any external authority figure.

❑ I am comfortable being alone and enjoy my own company more than chit chat.

❑ Conversations that explore the depths of an issue have meaning. I would rather have one deep meaningful conversation a day than twenty casual ones.

❑ I hold things in and don't allow others to see how I truly feel about something unless I'm certain it will be well received. I can be hard to get to know.

❑ Small dark spaces appeal to me more than large open spaces do. Small spaces feel snug and comforting, large spaces feel vulnerable and risky.

Five element charts

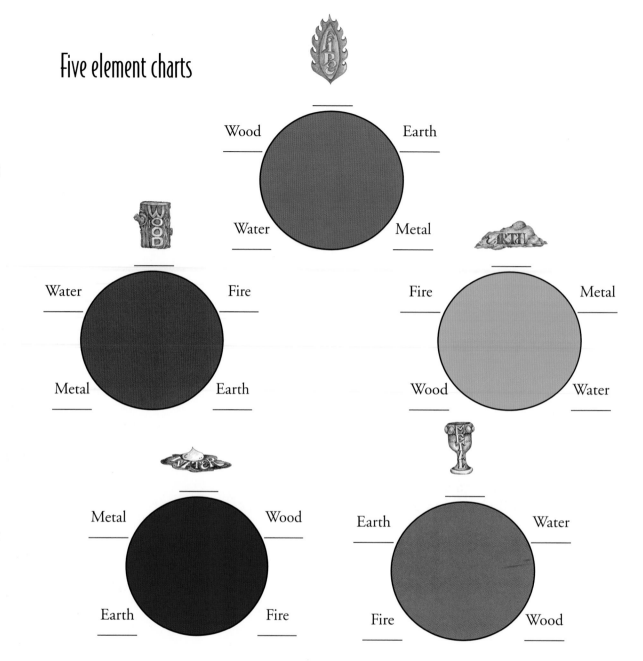

Finding your core element

Total the points for each type separately, adding or subtracting as you go. For example, if the scores in your Type A (Water) section were:

+1, +2, -1, -1, -1, +1, +1, +2, +2, -1,

your total score for that section would be +5. Now add your points in each of the other four sections. Once your have all five totals, find the circle for the element with your highest score at the top. If your highest score was Fire, place your Fire score on the top line of the circle which has Fire at the top. Then fill in your other scores in the order shown around the Fire circle. In this case, Fire is your core. Once you know your core element, use the charts on the following page to see which elements support your element and which ones weaken it. As you read through the book associated with each element, pay close attention to your core element. Increase design choices that strengthen and/or balance your core.

Adventure & productivity –the Wood kitchen

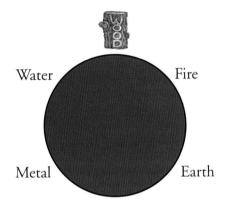

Water — Fire

Metal — Earth

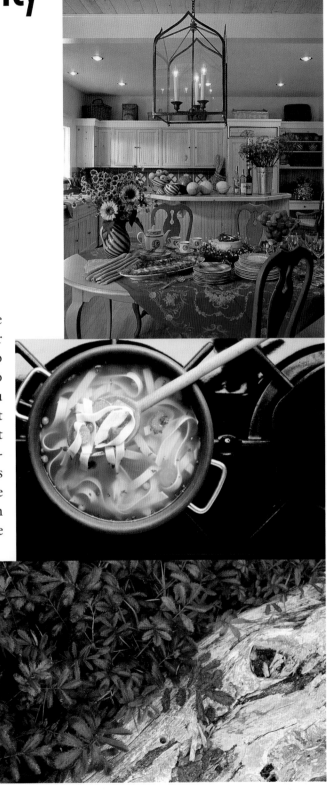

You wake with the dawn and waste no time lying in bed. You're up and making coffee or brushing your teeth, the first action of many to follow in the course of a normal day. Before too long, something captures your attention, and you dive into it with energy and enthusiasm. It might not be what you had planned to do that day, but the moment takes hold of you. Unfinished projects lay forgotten, while this new interest seizes your time and attention. You have no trouble organizing a force of helpful people to aid you in achieving your desired goal and naturally fill the role of leader and advisor. Annoyances and frustrations arise when you find others unable to accomplish assignments as quickly as you would have or when they don't grasp your meaning at the lightening speed at which you operate. Your tendency is to hurry up and do things yourself rather than slow down to the pace required to teach someone else how to do it. Lunch breaks and other normal rest times are opportunities to get one more thing done, and it's easy for you to regard others as lazy or perhaps just slow.

40

Wood energy in the kitchen

If you have a lot of Wood energy, you like to get up and get going in the morning, so a kitchen with eastern light is ideal. Your best work is often done before noon, and eastern kitchens are active from the hours of 6 a.m. to 11 a.m. Whether you choose to work in your kitchen or not, it is often the place you begin your day, think about what you want to do, and make your plans, so it sets the tone for you. If you have no access to eastern light in your kitchen, cut a window into an inside wall and bring in light that way.

Avoid placing your kitchen in the center of the house. This placement will make Wood energy feel boxed in and limited. As a result, you can begin to act in such as way as to actually attract obstacles and delays into your life, frustrating you and making it difficult to successfully complete your projects.

Placing the kitchen on the west side of the house can contribute to a sluggish start in the morning, and since you do your best work then, you can often feel as if you've wasted the entire day. Compensate for a western kitchen by making certain that a room you use early in the morning is on the east side of the house. You might need to change bedrooms, or turn a bedroom into an office.

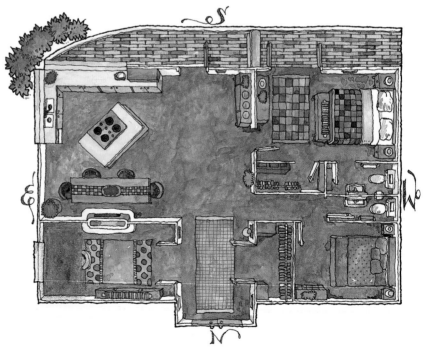

The eastern windows in this floor plan let early morning sunlight into the kitchen. The dining area falls into the Family/Ancestors area of the house, encouraging cross-generational connections and strong family ties.

Eastern energy

The east is associated with new growth, the birth of each new day, renewed energy and vigor, and budding optimism about future possibilities. Spend time in the east when you want to be motivated to take action.

Wood's goal:

Create a kitchen that allows activity and receives the eastern early morning light. Use tall vertical windows or enhance views of tall trees.

How Wood interacts with other elements

Wood energy gets things done. No idea or insight, no matter how great and noble, can affect change in the world unless someone acts on that idea. All the other elements need Wood's ability to take action. They count on you to stay motivated and full of drive. You count on them to come up with more great ideas, clean up your mess, take care of the details, and provide funding. When they don't, you feel unappreciated and stifled. Your challenge will be to recognize and honor that the contributions of others are as valuable as your own, and that without them, all your action would lead to nothing but exhaustion.

This kitchen's strong vertical window lines enhance the wooden cabinetry, creating a primarily Wood energy kitchen. However, the considerable doses of sunlight, fresh flowers, and colorful dishes all bring in Fire, while the granite countertops add the stability of Earth. This flow of energy from Wood to Fire to Earth, follows the constructive cycle of the elements, which raises the level of energy in both the home and its owners.

Wood's gift

Knowing how to do something is Wood's greatest gift. Our generation has lost touch with the rewards of being capable and self-sufficient. Excite the Wood energy in you by learning how to put together a shelf, bake bread from scratch, or become computer-literate.

Don't forget your children. They also need to feel capable. If they aren't needed at home, they tend to form their own groups where they can prove their value and swear their allegiance. Set up your home so that your children know they contribute to the family's success. By age six, children can sort laundry and fold clothes. Ten-year-olds can make a simple dinner and mow the lawn. When things break down, do your children know how to fix them? Do you? Get Wood. It gets the job done!

Wood with Fire—

Your energy is focused on doing, which finds its fulfillment in the external world, the realm of Fire. You want others to appreciate your efforts, indeed, others often appreciate your accomplishments more than you can yourself. You forge a path so others can follow you, which requires Fire's companionship and connection.

If your projects cannot find a voice in the external world, you feel like a failure and begin to flounder in your resolve. For all your inner drive, you crave External Recognition that you are valuable.

The tall vertical bar stools and the rounded column bring Wood energy into this social center. While square pillars should be avoided, rounded pillars create a link between heaven and earth, joining transformative and expansive Fire energy with practical grounding Earth energy. Creating this bridge between heaven and earth is Wood energy's job.

You can support Wood by adding Earth. Anytime you display a collection, you are increasing Earth.

Wood with Earth—

You have a hard time with Earth energy people who are constantly backtracking to make certain that everyone is okay. This seems like a huge waste of time to you, as you expect others to take care of their own needs as you take care of yours. While you need Earth's supporting comfort, you resist it at the same time, fearing that you will be drawn into a false sense of security and lose your drive. Earth's other gift, containment, is likewise a mixed blessing. You both need and fear this, knowing it can ground but also limit your projects.

Taking care of practical needs

Wood's penchant for doing things that have never been done before can make it easy to forget that you still live on planet Earth and have practical earthly needs. Let Earth support you in the following ways:

- **Remember to eat.**

- **Honor friendships and associations.**

- **Stay home at least one weekend a month.**

- **Spend time in your garden.**

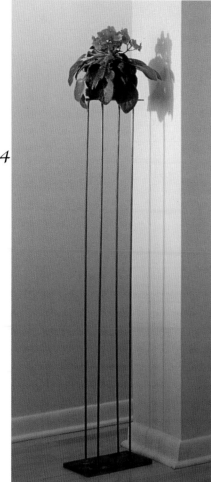

Wood with Metal—

Metal energy people can be difficult for you because they constantly remind you of the rules you should be following. You use rules as a guide, not a dictator, and have no problem breaking them if the situation warrants. However, with your tendency to be drawn from project to project, Metal helps you stay focused and stay on track. Without Metal, it's hard for you to finish projects.

above: This tall metal plant stand is a simple yet elegant example of a Wood/Metal combo. The plant helps soften the sharp metal lines of the stand, while the stand's very sharpness helps focus both the eye and the mind.

right: One of the easiest ways to bring Wood and Metal together is to paint your wood white. Just by changing the color, you bring order and structure to Wood's strength and drive.

Combining Wood with Water can be as simple as using tall goblets for water glasses. Remember, the more water you drink, the more your body wants to take action. There is no better way to fuel yourself than to drink a lot of water.

Wood with Water–

You appreciate Water's insights and use them to fuel your projects. By listening to Water, you can use Wood's directive force to shape your life around your inner truth. Water people need to move slowly, however, so guard against irritation and allow their spiritual depth to provide the bigger picture you need to find meaning in the many things you do throughout the day.

Water therapy for Wood

Water can soothe Wood's frustrated soul. Try the following on days when you tend to take on more projects than you can handle:

Wash your hands. This will draw toxins out of your body and relax you.

Soak your hands in warm water to soothe and calm your spirit. If you don't enjoy doing dishes, soak your hands in warm water or getting a paraffin wax treatment.

Pool water. A bowl of clean clear water in the kitchen represents your ability to "pool" (gather to yourself and hold onto) all of the earth's precious resources. For specific blessings, place small objects in the water that symbolize the resource you desire. For example, if you need more grounding and stability, place small stones in the water. If you need financial help, place coins in the water. If it's renewed health you desire, float a branch from a green plant or a budding flower in the bowl.

Wood's advice

Wood is the body's natural remedy for paralyzing and deadening depression. For people who aren't financially forced to go to work every day, luxury can become a curse. With nothing to motivate action, no projects to finish, no clients to meet, no reason to get up in the morning, the body deflates like a balloon. After a period of reclining activity, simple actions require a huge amount of effort.

When sinking into this type of depression, take whatever action you can muster, however small the action may seem. The relief is in the act. Once you brush your teeth or comb your hair, the next action will present itself. Step by step, action by action, you can create meaning in your life.

Your mantra:
"I choose a meaningful life."

This glass etching of tall vertical trees encased in a wood frame is a strong Wood/Wood symbol. It's hard to slough off when you see this every morning. Wood's motto: Just do it!

Wood with Wood–

Although you understand Wood's energy because it is like you, you don't necessarily want to work with other Wood energy people on a daily basis. They tend to be involved in their own projects and don't look to you for guidance. Your natural tendency to be competitive surfaces when other Wood people are around. Your best relationship with Wood is to find a mentor who excels in your chosen area. Its drive and ability can then support your desires, not compete with them.

The horizontal artwork in this kitchen creates Earth energy and is a great way to ground excessive Wood. It reminds Wood that everything must be done in order and that things take time. If you've got a hasty "Wood" energy person running around your home, increase the Earth energy.

When Wood gets excessive

Excessive Wood energy leads to burnout and exhaustion. Too much Wood and you can't stop doing until your body forces you to drop. You also tend to get quite impatient and easily irritated with others. If it's time to tone down your Wood, consider the following adjustments:

Replace the desk. Put an easy chair in the kitchen instead.

Turn the phone ringer off. If it's the phone that's always pulling your attention, turn the ringer off for an hour a day.

Exchange vertical blinds for horizontal ones. Vertical movement generates Wood energy while horizontal movement strengthens Earth. Horizontal blinds, pictures, and furniture slow life down.

Make a list of helpful people. Wood energy often feels that it has to do everything itself because others either won't help, can't do things "right," or haven't been given a chance. Make a list of those you trust and who have offered their support and keep it by the phone.

Wood's daily practice

Ever wonder why Wood people avoid having a daily practice? Daily practices require consistent, dedicated effort which is not Wood's specialty. Wood is willing to work hard, but wants things to change fast. Slow consistent change is a stretch.

If you have a lot of Wood, incorporate daily practices that allow variety. For example, begin a practice of reading every day for half an hour, but don't limit yourself to one book. Read five books at once.

Spend thirty minutes every day with your children, but allow yourself to change the activity that you do together. The daily part of your commitment will strengthen your Metal and prevent your Wood from getting out of control.

What to include— activity center

Wood energy loves to get things done, find out what's going on in the world, and be productive. Activity energizes you and prepares you for the day. Increase the activity level of your kitchen in the following ways:

Cook new dishes. Wood loves trying something new. Stock the refrigerator and cupboards with everything you need to cook on the spot.

Place the herbs and spices within reach. They play an important role in the creative process. For Wood, cooking is a work of art. You may not know what you're going to make before it's done.

Opt for functional dishware. Things need to work well and have a practical use. Wood hates broken appliances.

Don't store leftovers. They will rot before you will eat them and make you feel guilty. You tire of the same thing easily and eating the same food day after day will make you feel that life is tedious.

Keep the microwave. You might find it makes the difference between eating and not eating. If things take too long, you just won't do it. It is better to eat microwave macaroni and cheese than live on chips and soda.

This family chose to remove a boring kitchen cupboard and replace it with a tall vertical wooden cabinet. The fun colorful dishes keep Wood from taking life too seriously.

Use tall vertical shapes. Pillars, posts, and ladder-back chairs create a Wood energy pattern and will strengthen your core.

Guard against electromagnetic fields. People with a lot of Wood tend to suffer from headaches and fatigue often. Watch where you place outlets and light switches and keep seating areas far away from them. Consider a cork floor to absorb this radiation.

Place things high on the wall. Wood wants to ascend, reaching up as high as possible into the heavens. If your pictures hang low on the wall with empty space above, your natural tendency to soar will droop. Avoid anything on the floor that could trip you if you are not looking down.

Without appearing messy, this kitchen makes things easy to reach. Open shelving for storing bowls and pull-out wicker baskets for smaller items, a cutting board, and visible dishware, all cater to Wood's hurried pace.

This kitchen could easily be a home office. The TV provides easy news coverage, there's a chair for reading, notepad and pencils are right next to the phone, and the cooking utensils and spices are visible and handy.

Use natural wood. It encourages hard work and exertion, honors craftsmanship, and is limitless in its expression.

Use bamboo. Just like Wood, bamboo can be turned into flooring, window coverings, or furniture. Set your table with bamboo place mats or replace an existing cupboard with a bamboo cabinet.

Use a variety of distinctive woods, such as hickory or pine. Wood with variation in color and texture emphasizes the wood itself rather than its function as a cupboard, or a drawer.

Use untraditional colors and materials. Wood hates doing the same thing everyone else is doing. Tear down the old barn and turn it into your kitchen table. Paint your walls brilliant green. Try a bamboo floor or a varnished cork backsplash. Do whatever new and novel idea catches your attention. But, don't be surprised if you find you tire of things easily.

50

Keep things accessible. It is more important to have appliances within arm's reach than it is to have a spotless, clutter-free countertop. Speed and ease are your top priorities.

Create an expansive view. Oversized windows can lift and open a view that might otherwise constrict. Consider paintings that depict vistas, landscapes, or oceans to balance out small windows or depressing views. Plant a tree outside your window, so that even if your view is limited, your eye moves up to the sky.

Have a cordless phone. The phone allows you to be in more than one place at once and get things done.

Remove the television. This passive activity will make Wood feel frustrated.

Be certain the kitchen is spacious. A small closed-off kitchen will depress your spirits and darken your hopes.

Increase Wood by placing something on the wall above your doors to catch the eye and lift the chi. The placement of this "It's a Wonderful Life" wall plaque draws the eye upward, creating a rising (Wood vibration) chi in the body.

Allow for activity. Anything that allows your chi to move is good. This could be a computer center where you can log on to the internet and send a quick e-mail or set up a meeting for later in the day, or it could be a tall kitchen island that allows you to stand and eat.

Connection & sensuality
—the Fire kitchen

For the Fire personality, a good day is a day full of people, sensual experiences, and the sensation of transcendence. Just walking down the street or sitting in your cubicle at work brings a cacophony of stimuli. You seem to feel what everyone around you is feeling. When they come to tell you of their difficulties, you burden your heart and struggle to find a way to help them. Because you tend to do this on a regular basis, you can become beset and overwhelmed by other people's feelings, yet unable to detach yourself. You love beautiful things and laugh easily. In fact, nothing seems to get you down for

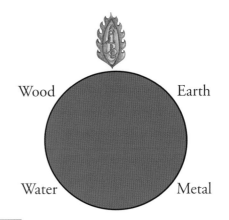

Wood   Earth

Water   Metal

long because you notice beauty and find humor in unlikely places. You tend to learn a little about everything without ever going too deep into any one thing. You have no fear of social settings and feel more comfortable with a lot of people around rather than being by yourself.

Southern energy

Southern energy will raise your heart rate, get your blood pumping, and lower your inhibitions. If you'd like a little more excitement in your life, spend more time in the south. If you've had a traumatic experience or feel emotionally vulnerable, avoid spending a lot of time in the south.

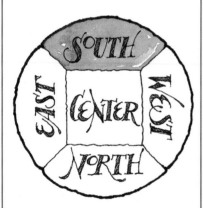

Fire's goal:

The bigger the better as far as your kitchen goes. Stay away from a narrow galley-style kitchen. Opt for a kitchen that expands onto a great room or social area.

Fire energy in the kitchen

You are a creature of intensity and passion. As such, you benefit from the southern sun's intense heat and bright light. Because your element is in danger of fast burnout, avoid placing stoves, ovens, and microwave ranges in the southern part of your kitchen or directly in view of large windows.

Surround Fire appliances with Earth energy in the form of granite or pottery and use tile on the floor. If your kitchen falls in another area of the house, make certain remodel plans include adding windows or skylights to increase sunlight.

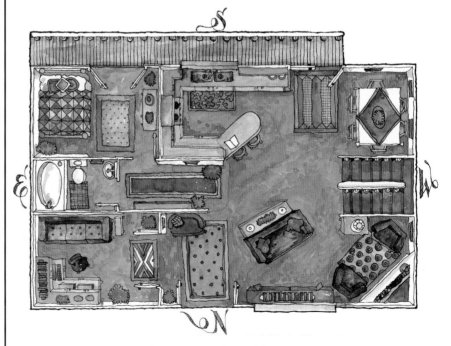

This floor plan capitalizes on the expansive chi of the south. Sliding doors onto a back deck expand the space visually and socially. The stove is placed on the east wall to temper excessive fire. The kitchen is open to both the great room and the dining area, with only a small separation between it and the entrance hall.

If you have a fiery personality and love colors and fun new things, you can still bring a little Water into your life hanging a colorful mobile. The downward moving energy of this mobile will help move your own energy down lower in your body, lessening Fire's frantic tendency and increasing Water's stillness.

Put your computer in the kitchen

As a Fire energy person, you won't want to do your bills in a back bedroom, shut off and isolated from everyone else. Use your kitchen remodel to get your computer out into the more social areas of the house. Plenty of small tucked away corners could be home to a built-in desk area. Try removing a wall and building in shelves above and a desk below. Putting a computer center near the kitchen can help you deal with your mail, pay your bills, and post family messages where they'll be seen. Just make certain to keep your new desk out of the work triangle and main walkways.

How Fire interacts with other elements

Fire energy is connection. Issues with feeling isolated, separate, rejected, and cut off from the group are Fire issues. The ability to rejoin and merge with a group or another person is Fire's gift. When you feel all alone, surround yourself with candles and allow the dancing flames to warm and open your heart center. Regardless of whether your external situation changes, you'll feel more connected.

Fire with Earth–

Although you love people and feel things intensely, Earth is more the caretaker than you are. Earth seems able to sustain the connections and relationships that flit by you in an instant. You connect; Earth keeps the connection alive. You constantly encourage Earth to try new things and explore the delights of the senses. Earth, in turn, encourages you to put down roots, pull your head out of the clouds and be practical.

You can shift the balance of any room by simply changing a few items. The top photo creates strong Fire energy. Roosters are Fire symbols, unabashedly singing to the entire world. Hot-chili peppers and bright intense colors also generate more Fire. Note also the picture of ripe fruit and the ceramic pig (live images).

To tone down the Fire in this corner and create Earth energy, we traded the chili peppers for a carved-out bowl. The candles were replaced with Earth colors and are not lit. We replaced the rooster with a basket of vegetables. The pig and picture of fresh fruit were replaced with a vase and a bowl (two more containers). The colors in general went from bright intense reds to soft subdued pinks and browns.

Fire with Metal–

Prepare for long list of rules and regulations. You shirk off policy and procedure. Caution and precision are antithetical to your very being. You want to feel, to open, to push the envelope, to transcend limits and boundaries. Metal wants to enforce rules, strengthen boundaries, and cut off emotions (as they tend to interfere with reason). You and Metal can learn to respect each other, but you'll never want the same things.

If your Fire energy demands that you have place settings for twenty, find a way to keep them organized. The kitchen below is the perfect balance of Fire and Metal. The Fire element shows with the high ceilings, ample tableware, copper pots, fresh flowers, and sunny windows. The Metal element is represented through the white cupboards and the pure cleanliness.

Fire with Water–

You and Water are opposites. You want to go out, Water wants to stay home and read. You tend to make decisions quickly, Water takes forever. You love the pleasures of the physical body, Water doesn't seem to even know it has a body. You tend to always see the positive, Water is always pointing out the terrible things that could happen. If Water is a permanent member of your family, you two have some work to do. You'll need to spend some time alone, getting more comfortable with silence, and Water will need to consent to coming out with you once in awhile.

This U-shaped cook island successfully separates the guests from the cook. Such containment represents the isolation Water seeks.

Black granite countertops help Water energy feel comfortable in a social situation.

To enter the cook's domain one must pass through a relatively narrow portal, preventing all but the most intrusive guest from coming into the cook's kitchen.

Wood and Fire make a great combination. Fire brings Wood's projects out into the external world and helps Wood connect and share its enthusiasm with others. This wooden candleholder is a perfect symbol of Wood and Fire in balance, holding, not just one, but six candles.

Fire with Wood–

Wood's ideas and projects fuel your passion. You get excited about plans and possibilities, but tend not to follow through on things the way you thought you would. Wood is fearless, and you like that, but Wood can also be heartless and selfish, and you tend to bear the brunt of his ability to close up quickly. In fact, Wood is a puzzle, open and warm one minute, closed and aloof the next. What you don't realize is that your intensity scares Wood and, although it desires the fulfillment and passion that Fire brings, it also fears losing itself in the flames.

Fire's gift

Fire loves to entertain. You plan a romantic brunch for Sunday morning, the kind of event other people only read about. Wine, fresh flowers, music, great food, all delight and bring out the best in Fire. Use this natural ability to enhance the other aspects of your life. If you're working on a project (Wood energy) and others are getting stressed, invite them over for a work dinner, get them talking to each other, and help them relax. This is your gift.

Transcend the ordinary

Fire with Fire—

Watch out world. When two Fire energy people get together, there's nothing to stop their heat from building. They can experience indescribable passion and moments of transcendence, but they can't seem to hold onto it. If your encounters with other Fire energy people get too intense, subdue the flames by taking a time-out day in between meetings.

This large open room is Fire's ideal social center. There are no boundaries between the kitchen and the living area. The double islands, double sink areas, and double refrigerators allow multiple cooks to work together smoothly. The five-foot wide passageways facilitate traffic flow even with forty or more people in the space. The red cabinetry keeps the atmosphere festive. Everywhere you look there are pictures and dishes with animals on them, and with twenty separate lights, you can create any mood you desire.

When the Fire energy in your home gets excessive, your cravings might get excessive too. Since Fire energy stimulates the senses, reducing Fire can help you get food and alcohol cravings back under control.

When Fire gets excessive

If you have trouble separating your emotions from others', you might need to put out some Fire. Too much Fire feels everything, causing physical illness or anxiety attacks. Lessen these tendencies by performing the following adjustments:

Keep a journal about your feelings. This is a helpful way of learning to separate your own emotions from others'. Although you don't naturally pause to think about yourself and how you feel, you will find the journal helps you get things out so you can relax.

Place alcohol and other stimulants out of sight. To stimulate your body when you are already suffering from excessive heat will make it more difficult to return to balance.

Lower shades and dim lights. Although you tend to crave light, spending time in a cool dimly lit room can restore much-needed balance. Try dimming lights in the evening before retiring to bed to ease you into a calmer, more relaxed state.

Add black accessories. Black can be strong medicine for someone with no boundaries. Wear black, try black cushions on your bar stools, or drink from a black cup.

Put a cork in it

If you're bubbling over, try adding cork to your kitchen. Soft underfoot, cork flooring is absorbing and yin in nature. It will soften the shocks of the day and help you to settle down. Cork doesn't readily conduct heat or cold, so it stays room temperature. One more virtue, cork absorbs sound, a must for households with many children or with living areas underneath the kitchen. It's also made from bark, so it doesn't destroy the forests.

What to include—a social hub

You need a large kitchen. Because you love social gatherings, and kitchens make every gathering more social, building a kitchen large enough to accommodate guests is essential. In fact, the preparation of the food itself becomes part of the socializing in your kitchen.

Include a stereo. A quiet house makes you feel uncomfortable. Whether you listen to music or the song of birds, you'll feel more alive with music.

Activate all the senses. Sights, smells, and tastes are all important. The more active your senses, the more alive you feel. Food needs to do more than taste good. It needs to be served on a beautiful plate, with a contrasting yet elegant napkin.

Two or three different glasses hold water, wine, and additional refreshment, and you take the time to light the candles, turn on music, and open the window for the evening breeze.

Choose dishes for the visual impact, rather than functionality. Functional is fine, as long as it's beautiful, but you'd rather put up with impractical stunning dishes than eat on boring plates.

Buy in bulk. You're more likely to invite a gathering of eight than you are two or three. Buying bulk will save money and help reduce Fire's tendency to drain a budget. Be careful though, sometimes buying in bulk can lead to wasting in bulk.

Fresh flowers and ripe fruit bring pleasure and elevate your mood. Summer, the Fire time of year, is the season of fullness.

60

Taken from the kitchen counter, this photo illustrates how everything is open in a Fire house. From the large windows to the open floor plan, this Fire house makes it easier for people to connect with each other. It is difficult to feel "left out" or alone in this home.

Bar stools make it easy to slip in and out of conversations and keep socializing light and fun, which is always Fire's goal.

Have an expansive sunny view. Fire energy does not like to feel contained, expansive views make you feel as if your ability to grow, create, and live were endless.

Use radiant heat, rather than forced air. Although you will want to avoid radiant heat that runs underneath the entire floor, you can use radiant baseboard heating or other forms of radiant heat that do not pass moving water directly underneath where people will be standing or sitting.

Support & comfort—the Earth kitchen

Your day probably starts with remembering that you need to call so-and-so and make certain they know about the neighborhood or family gathering coming up. Then it's off to the kitchen to make a big breakfast for whoever might be staying in the house at the time, even though you may not ever sit down to eat yourself. As the one who holds everything and everyone together, your day is filled with thoughts of others. You wonder about how they're feeling, what they're doing, what they might need, and how you might help them. You remember the birthday of a friend that you haven't seen for over ten years and you find the time to call a neighbor and ask how her son's surgery went.

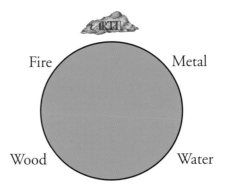

It is your constancy that allows for smooth transitions. As the seasons change from yin to yang and back, they pass through an Earth cycle, needing her grounding and stabilizing force. Your stabilizing abilities can take the form of scheduling someone else's day for them, creating comforting places to live in, sheltering others from someone's wrath or caustic nature, or using positive words to strengthen a floundering self-esteem. You contain chaos, soften jaggedness, and provide a sense of belonging.

Central energy

Regain control over your center. If the physical center of your home is a bathroom or closet, work with the center of the kitchen. In the kitchen, be certain you can stand comfortably in the center (don't place an island or a kitchen table here). Position things so when you stand in the center, you can see other areas of the house.

Use a large circular rug to mark the center of the room. Anything you can reach from the rug is pulled into your center. If you have a lighting fixture in the center of the kitchen, link your personal chi to the chi of the light. As light radiates out and fills your space, your energy will travel to expand your center.

Earth's goal:
To continually balance out conflicting energies.

Earth energy in the kitchen

Earth energy is the center of everything. You are not content to sit around on the periphery, you are the heart of the home and family gatherings. Everyone counts on you to pull it altogether and make things happen. If the kitchen, the most important room for nurturing and supporting others, is positioned off to the side, it interferes with your natural abilities and tendencies. Your family loses a sense of center and your role of stabilizing and balancing the comings and goings of the house is disrupted. If you can't physically be in the center in your home, your own internal sense of balance can be disturbed. You might feel dizzy or out-of-sorts. If you can't return to center often, you'll struggle to maintain a sense of purpose and value.

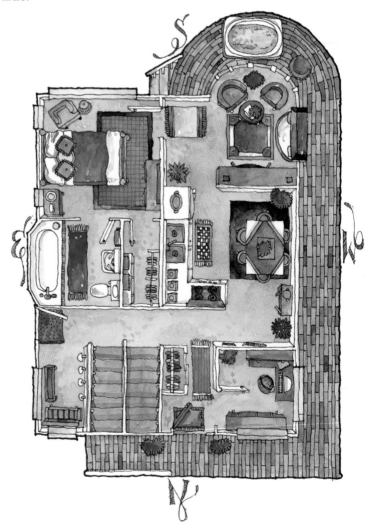

The Earth house places the kitchen in the center of the home. Although there's not much living space, as evidenced in this two-bedroom house, things feel comfortable and welcoming.

64

The desk to the left is set up to support an Earth energy person.

- **knicknacks & containers**
- **photographs of loved ones**
- **soft padded seat**

As shown below, the same desk area can be changed to suit the needs of a Wood energy person.

- **tall plants**
- **day planner**
- **shelf full of books**
- **tall & wooden chair**

How Earth interacts with other elements

In essence, your tremendous ability to give and support others defines all your relationships. The well of your strength and kindness seems endless, but as your giving becomes expected by those around you, and they turn to you again and again, you can feel drained and exhausted. You desire relationships that allow you to support the efforts of others and receive loving support in return.

Contain your Earth

Earth wants to be certain there is enough for everyone to enjoy. If you have this tendency, make your food storage visually pleasant. Use colored-glass jars or mix and match sizes and containers to keep your collections interesting. Finding the right containers can turn a mess into a delight.

You can store Earth's abundance if you invest in some of these contemporary cupboards. The ability to organize, separate, and categorize is Metal's gift. With slide-out drawers, these cabinets allow you to stay organized while indulging in Earth's need to see everything. Want to know what's on shelf three? Pull it out and have a look!

Earth with Metal–

Earth's tendency to collect and gather things creates a strong need for Metal's ability to structure and organize. Without Metal to prune what Earth gathers, Earth can get more and more stuck, bogged down with too much stuff, and become a prisoner to things. Metal can slice through, cut off and let go of what's no longer needed. You might resist Metal's seeming lack of concern, but you grow by learning to let your Earth energy pass into a Metal phase. Let Metal help you clean your house, get organized, and create structure for your day.

Earth with Water–

You are of this world, Water lives in the world of spirit. Waters' refusal to take care of their practical needs can sometimes drive you crazy, and you might find yourself caretaking them; however, they also can offer you gifts. When Earth hardens and loses its ability to move and be flexible, Water softens it again. Likewise, when you get stuck in your ways or consumed by your daily routine, Water can help you step out of your day-to-day life and see the bigger picture.

Both Water and Earth love writing letters. It's a wonderful way to stay nestled up in bed and still connect with loved ones.

Find your center

Think about what you can reach from the center of your kitchen. Can you reach the phone? If so, that strengthens your ability to reach out and connect with others. Can you reach the stove? If so, that strengthens your ability to nurture and support others physically. Can you reach the sink? If so, you can symbolically nurse others' wounds and, through the art of cleansing, reduce the possibility of illness and disease. Can you reach the pantry and cupboards? If so, you have the ability to store nutrients and resources for a time of need. By strengthening the center, you strengthen your Earth.

67

Controlling paper

Has paper taken over your counters? Containers are the key! As much as Earth likes to gather things, Earth also loves to give things a home. Valuing home is why Earth loves containers so much. Use this to your advantage. Go get half a dozen in & out baskets. These are now available in wood, woven grasses, all kinds of styles that will work in a kitchen as well as in the office. They are open on the top and stack, one on top of the other. Stack them two high, anymore than that and the top basket will be overflowing while the others remain empty. Use one for personal mail, one for current bills, another for interesting ideas and articles, perhaps an entire basket for medical concerns, you get the idea. Once things have a home, the fog in your brain will lift and you'll feel more capable to handle your day.

Earth with Wood—

Although this person desperately needs your balancing and stabilizing presence, they're probably the last to admit it. As you struggle to give them the support and grounding they need to flourish, they must strain against your boundaries in order to grow. This interaction is epitomized by adolescent children and the supportive parents. The more parents offer to support their children, the more children must strike out on their own in order to find out who they are and what they want to do in the world. Your task here is to refrain from mothering or worrying about Wood, knowing that the more they grow up and away from you, the deeper they plant their roots in your soil.

In this old-fashioned farm-style kitchen, everything centers around a large table for eight. Placing a workspace at the center is a great way to move Earth energy into a more active Wood phase. Your family will be more active seated at a table rather than cuddled up on a couch.

Eating areas, such as this breakfast nook, increase Earth by holding energy in and allowing it to settle down. Even padding your chairs and throwing a pillow on a bench can soften and bring comforting Earth energy to your kitchen.

Earth with Fire–

As Fire burns down it creates ashes, or Earth. Thus Fire energy naturally turns to Earth when it has exhausted itself. This pattern can manifest in many ways. You could find yourself cleaning up after Fire energy makes a mess (Fire loves to entertain and throw lavish parties). Perhaps you create the cozy sitting area that family and friends crash in after a day of shopping. More likely, you'll find your Fire friends come to you to help them stabilize their emotions. Fire feels everything intensely and it needs you to siphon the drama off the latest event and reassure it that everything will be okay.

Earth's tendencies

- You love to collect things.

- You value long-term relationships.

- You are the memory-maker, taking pictures and telling stories of the past.

- You avoid conflict and always keep the peace.

- You think of others first, rather than yourself.

- Comfort is more important than cleanliness.

- You crave sugar, breads, and sweet things.

Nurturing relationships

Earth energy is at the heart of your relationships. It represents commitment to something greater than yourself. Home symbols, such as a wood carving, remind you of your commitment to honor and find value in your partner.

Earth with Earth—

Earth with Earth can settle in for a good long season of mutual caretaking. You love to hang out with other Earth people because you know that only they will notice and take care of your needs. Always the one who gives and cares for others, you need Earth to give back and care for you. Isn't it nice when someone forces you to stop your chores and takes you to lunch? Isn't it a great friend who buys you a gift certificate for a massage or a pedicure, knowing you would never do that for yourself? Earth friends make great fellow collectors and fellow worrywarts. As a caution, make certain the two of you don't feed each other's tendency to worry. Resist the impulse to sit around concocting hypothetical scenarios.

The thick walls and window casements in this straw-bale house increase a feeling of safety and security.

This is an example of Earth's tendency to smother—too many books, too many pillows, no space for walking, all indicate excessive Earth.

When Earth gets excessive

Excessive Earth typically manifests as unmanageable clutter or constant worrying. When energy can't move, it stagnates. Stagnant Earth energy finds itself unable to let go of things, even if they no longer serve a purpose. You might be keeping magazines or newspapers that are outdated. You might have furniture or personal items from relatives who have passed on that you have no room for or reason to keep. You might find yourself worrying about people and things that you have no control over or ability to help. However it manifests in your life, draining excessive Earth can be accomplished in the following ways:

Work away worry. If you find yourself continually worrying, engage in a Wood activity such as gardening. Try an indoor herb garden, or repotting existing plants. Don't let plants sit in plastic pots; buy terra-cotta pots and rich soil. Give Earth energy a constructive focus, and you'll find the time and energy you spend worrying diminishes.

Collect containers

Earth loves collecting items and using containers. Since Earth energy holds and gathers, containers are a natural extension of an Earth personality. Use your love of containers to bring in Metal and help organize.

Sort. To get rid of unnecessary things, go through a Metal phase and decide what has value to your present life and what does not. Realize the last thing you feel like doing is organizing. Then know that the next step in the normal cycle of life is to sort through and organize the things that you have been accumulating.

What to include—the traditional hearth

Display your collections. As a chi gatherer, you tend to collect things. Display collections in an orderly fashion so that you honor both the items themselves and your own need for organization. Whether it's teapots, photographs, spoons, or china, you'll feel stuck if you let it get out of hand.

Use muted or grayed colors. Earth is not bright, new, or shiny, but has the worn patina of years of use. If you like green, try a sage or olive green. If you want red, use a muddy brick red, not scarlet or crimson. Grayed blues, browns, terra-cotta, and yellows will strengthen Earth energy.

Give yourself a place to sit. The Earth kitchen is a gathering place. This is not where you will have a single chair off in a corner. Bring the couch in, or tear down a wall so those seated on the sofa in the living room can see into and be a part of what's happening in the kitchen.

Don't be afraid of antiques. Earth energy respects and anchors to the past, but antiques carry as much negative energy as they do positive. If you have a piece bringing troublesome energy into your home, clear the negative chi by submerging it in rock salt or washing it with a mixture of vinegar and water. If the piece is made of wood, use linseed oil with lemon.

Surround yourself with family. Display pictures or heirloom dishes, and have plenty of chairs for family to gather.

Creating intentional displays for your collections, such as this wine cellar, honors both you and the collection. Piles of unsorted photographs don't serve anyone. Neither do stacks of china hidden in a box in the basement. Finding just the right way to display your things can make all the difference between being overwhelmed or delighted by them.

72

Preparing Earth

Stock cupboards and refrigerator. As soon as you know everyone has what they need, you can relax. Make it easy on yourself by preparing for possibilities before they arise. This gives you a sense of comfort in knowing that, whatever happens, you're prepared.

Stocking and prepping beforehand will help you relax, since you'll know that, no matter what unexpected thing happens, you have enough for everyone.

Round corners and soft seats. Earth energy loves protection and safety. Sharp edges are warning signals and cause us to move with caution, which weaken Earth.

Use horizontal objects and surfaces to ground and balance volatile energy patterns. These can also lower the energy of a vaulted ceiling to make the space more comfortable.

Create a recycling center. Earth energy cares for and protects the natural resources. Always worried about what might happen in the future, Earth people reuse, store, and recycle just as the physical earth does. Setting up your kitchen—a site of much potential waste—in a way that allows you to recycle and reuse the earth's resources will help you feel that your own needs will be taken care of and that there will be enough in the future.

Thick walls, such as these exposed straw bales, hold and comfort like nothing else. Like the earth, they hold energy in and absorb the shock and stress of life's daily events.

Order & cleanliness
—the Metal kitchen

Earth Water

Fire Wood

You wake as soon as the alarm goes off, perhaps even a few minutes before. You've already planned your day the night before, and you know what you need to get ready to best approach the day's tasks. Your kitchen operates like a Swiss clock. Cupboards are organized, everything has a place and a container. Things are grouped by category, (you wouldn't dream of putting breakfast cereals on the same shelf as baking supplies) and there's a logical, almost scientific quality to your ordering.

Labeling machines were invented for you. You seem to process life with your head, rather than your body, thinking things through rather than feeling your way through. You are solution-oriented more than problem-oriented, and once you find the best way of doing something, you tend to do it that way from then on.

If you are the parent, your Metal energy makes it easy for you to discipline your children in a consistent manner. If, however, your children have stronger Metal energy than you, you'll find they are often chiding you or telling you the way things should be.

Western energy

The west is active later in the day. If your time to relax and share a meal with family and friends comes after work, consider a western kitchen.

The challenge in a Metal personality's kitchen is that Metal is mental, not physical, and is concerned more with process and procedure than with physical nourishment. Cooking food often requires making a mess, which doesn't sit well with Metal.

The time of day that Metal finds easiest to cook is early evening, when the workday is done and distractions are put away. If the kitchen can capture a view of a sunset, it might have a strong enough pull to get Metal out of a school book and into a cookbook.

Metal's goal:
    Get organized.

Metal energy in the kitchen

Metal's capacity to discern aligns with the compass direction of the west. Discernment comes after much experience, and this is represented by Metal's association with evening, autumn, and later life. When the sun is in the west, it's a natural time of gathering. We gather together with our families. We make certain our animals are in for the night or gathered together in a corral or barn. We mentally gather together the various parts of the day and work to make sense of our experiences. If we are facing a westward direction when performing these gathering types of activities, it will strengthen our natural abilities.

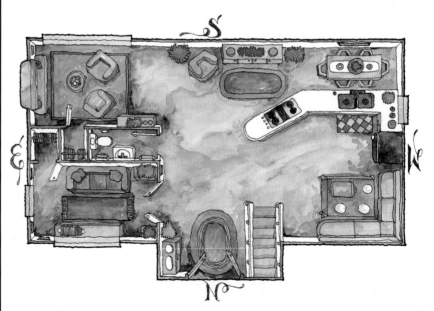

With a western window letting in chi, this kitchen will come alive after 5 p.m. The Metal kitchen has lots of dividers and cupboards for storage, and everything gets put away after use. Because the kitchen falls in the Creativity/Children area of the house, you'll be more inclined to cook creatively here.

How Metal interacts with other elements

Metal is always trying to make sense out of what the other elements are up to. It distills Water's mysteries. It puts a time line on Wood's projects. It finds a pattern in Fire's chaotic movements. It uncovers Earth's treasures. Metal's refining organizing strength is what keeps chaos from overwhelming our daily lives. Unfortunately, the other elements don't always take kindly to Metal's meddling. Metal needs to remember that rules and systems exist to serve people, not the other way around.

Curved counters, stainless steel, and the lack of handles on the cupboards identifies the Metal kitchen above. Although this kitchen captures sunlight and a view of trees outside, both of which soften a strong Metal energy, the Metal energy in this lower view of the same kitchen feels excessive. Simply adding a few plants or freshly cut flowers would take the edge off and make the entire room more comfortable.

The Metal kitchen prizes efficiency. This kitchen was designed to allow the owner's to load the dishwasher while still seated at the table. That way there is no added work or messy counters.

Metal is not one to admire a garbage can, so slide-out cupboards that completely hide any sign of garbage are ideal.

These metal spoons are hung as a mobile. The mobile's downward moving energy shifts Metal into a Water phase.

Metal with Water—

Your tendency to think things through and attend to all the details leads straight to Water. Pulling things together, integrating them and synthesizing your many experiences often leads to a deeper awareness or greater level of consciousness. This emergence into the deep triggers a Water phase. You might find your ability to put everything together in an organized systematic way is just what your friends need to reach the insights associated with Water energy. Since deep water can get murky, especially if it stagnates, your ability to refine and find the essence of something can gift Water with some much needed clarity.

Metal with Wood–

Like Wood, you like getting things done, but Wood's constant need to do things his own way and try out new ideas is problematic. To you, it simply makes sense that things should be done using methods that have been tried and proven effective. Wood also refuses to recognize and respect authority figures and considers himself beyond the reach of the law. Of course, you know that no one is "beyond" reach and Wood is only fooling himself. In fact, you might place yourself in a position to enforce rules and regulations, whether it's as a school crossing guard, a laboratory assistant, or a hospital nurse.

Eliminating cupboards is a way to simplify your life. The owner of this kitchen intentionally chose open shelving, encouraging simplicity and reducing clutter.

Green and white is a perfect color scheme for Metal who needs Wood's influence. The white keeps the kitchen feeling clean and tidy, the green constantly encourages movement and growth. The wood paneling halfway up the wall is another growth catalyst, but notice the Metal influence in the tidy way everything is stored.

Eliminate unnecessary and costly hardware by carving grooved handles into kitchen drawers. The look appeals to Metal's fondness for a smooth surface.

Metal with Fire–

Order and organization get thrown to the winds by Fire energy. More concerned with people than process, and unable to see how process can help and support people, Fire is a wild card in your plans. You dislike Fire's inconsistency and constantly changing moods. Where you seek to create clarity, definition, and boundaries, Fire seeks to obliterate any distinction. Merging is what Fire is after, a transformative blending of energies. Such merging is your greatest fear since it destroys the very categories by which you order your life and create meaning.

To keep life's excitement use colorful, imaginative containers for storage.

This hand-blown fixture of Venetian glass brings Metal's affinity for circles together with Fire's fondness for a kaleidoscope of color. The blending colors soften Metal's rigidity and whisper, "relax and enjoy."

Metal with Earth–

A strong mother figure to all, Earth is especially important to you. It initiates the gathering process that draws things together, helping them coalesce. You then take this inward-moving energy and use it to discern the essence of any life situation. Your ability to focus energy and understand how things work together transforms Earth's pile of seemingly unrelated components into an understandable, organized group or system.

This handy drawer puts Metal to work organizing an Earth person's spice collection. While Earth tends to throw all the spices into a drawer, Metal divides things into categories and creates order out of chaos. The separate rows and upturned labels are a sure sign that a Metal person has been here.

In an otherwise minimalist kitchen, the owners chose to install a professional wok. This decision has supported their personal commitment to eat fresh foods, not processed garbage. Because the wok is always visible and handy, they find they use it almost daily.

Metal with Metal–

Spending time with other Metal people increases your focus and powers of discernment. You can both respect the intelligence and insights of the other person, and benefit from having Metal energy people as mentors and colleagues. Avoid too many Metal friends though, or you'll experience an increasing tendency to be sarcastic and sharp with those who seem slow or less capable than yourself.

The photographs above and to the right reveal how small changes can make a difference in adding comfort to a Metal energy room.

- Add live plants.

- Fill a vase with fresh flowers.

- Display nuts and fruit on the counters.

- Cover the concrete floor with a rug.

- Add colored dishes.

When Metal gets excessive

Excessive Metal energy manifests as a cold, uninviting, sterile environment. When this happens in your home, it's likely to affect your relationships by feeling sharp, sarcastic, biting, or simply cold and distant. The excessively Metal person begins to care more for process and procedure than they do about people.

Activate the senses, especially smell. Cook something with a strong aroma, mist your kitchen with scented water, or bring fresh flowers in and inhale deeply of their fragrance.

Choose a few items to leave out on your counters. Find something you use often; and display it in a way that makes it both functional as well as beautiful. Then you won't mind as much leaving it out.

Select a soft white rather than a cool white for walls or cupboards. Everyone will relax more and you'll feel less on edge yourself.

A strong Metal room is great for mental focus, but is not condusive for physical nourishment. This kitchen represents such strong Metal energy that it would be extremely difficult to relax in the room. Remember that the purpose of a kitchen is to nourish your body. Add some fresh fruits or vegetables, green plants, or colorful dish towels to soften the sharpness.

What to include—emulate a ship's galley

Your strong need for order and cleanliness make it imperative that your kitchen have a designated home for each cup, plate, utensil, and appliance. More than that, everything should get put away after each use, not left out just in case you might need it again someday. Dishes should go straight from the table to the dishwasher, not be left sitting on the counter or in the sink. The sink gets wiped out constantly to prevent spots and stains.

Plan for numerous cleaning stations. Meals can be messy and you like to get things clean as soon as possible. In fact, you often clean as you go, rinsing off a knife or cleaning the chopping board as soon as you're finished with it. You can't relax and enjoy a meal if the kitchen is a mess. If your kitchen is large, it can help to have more than one sink or dishwasher, depending on how many dishes need to get done all at once. Be certain your water areas are separated from and not directly across from your cooking areas.

Prioritize cleanliness over comfort. A clean polished feel will make your kitchen a place you want to be. Purchase appliances that are easy to clean and pans that wipe off without effort.

Paint cupboards or walls white. White represents cleanliness and purity, being without spot or stain. It can also make old surfaces look new again. Remember though, white increases mental intellectual energy. If you find you're already too Metal, use white sparingly.

Include actual metal. Metal is rigid and has well-defined boundaries. It can instill clarity and a strong sense of definition when a room starts to feel muddled. Stainless steel is good for Metal folks since it's both made from metal and polishes well.

The metal appliances, circular chair backs, minimalist décor, and sharp curves create a strong Metal energy in this kitchen.

Knife handling

Keep knives sharp and stored in a block or drawer where the blades don't touch. Knives are strong symbols of Metal energy in a kitchen. They cut through the fat and get right to the meat. Keeping them sharp represents a keen mind and great powers of induction.

Because knives are sharp, they need to be treated with respect and kept away from other knives. Too much sharpness together can create injury and weaken the physical body.

Keep things warm with copper. With your strong need for cleanliness, you might get accused of being sterile from time to time. Soften sterility by using warm metals, such as copper, in your décor.

Incorporate arcs into your kitchen. The shape of the arc represents the power of discernment and strengthens Metal energy. You can include arches in doorways, light fixtures, or trimwork.

Buy a stand for your cookbook. Metal plays by the rules, which means following directions, even from a cookbook. Metal gets good results by following recipes exactly and not leaving anything to chance or interpretation. A stand that allows you to read easily from your cookbook will make it easier for you to follow recipes and reduce the risk of failure.

Adopt a streamlined décor style. Too much stuff will feel awkward and confining. There's no need to display all your spices if you feel it junks up your counters. Since you're the type that remembers where you put things, it's okay to hide them behind cupboard doors.

The circular table and curved chairs bring communal energy into this kitchen.

Spirituality & inner depth— the Water kitchen

Linear time is not important to you. Often you're not certain what time it is or how long you've been sitting, reflecting, or pondering something. In fact, you're more likely to do your best work in the middle of the night or wee hours of the morning rather than between 8 a.m. and 5 p.m. The veil is thin between this world and other dimensions and you often feel as much a "spirit being" as you do a "physical being." Your domain is one of inactivity, yet infinite potential. You wait, wonder, and envision what is to come.

You spend your days quietly, often enjoying your own company for long periods of time. The desire to be "out there in the world" feels distant and strange to you. You wonder that the opinions of others can have such sway over some. Your decisions and opinions come from a deeper place, a well of wisdom that flows from a cosmic connection to the great Tao. Others envy your peaceful manner. Not much ruffles you. You always seem to grasp the bigger picture behind it all and can make sense of things for others. That is, if they'll listen to your quiet voice.

Time stands still. You are in the middle of a cosmic swirl of energy. There is nothing you must do, just be, and, sometimes painfully, return to the earth realm to share with others what you see.

Northern energy

The energy of the North is about slowing down and moving inward. This facilitates Water's tendency to be introspective, plumbing the darkness of night and the cold of winter for life's elusive secrets.

Water's goal:
Turn inward for answers to life;s questions.

Water energy in the kitchen

If you do your best work at night, don't fight it; learn to enjoy a midnight snack. The energy of the north is most active in the middle of the night and can energize you in a way that daylight can't. Your view of the moon is more important than watching the rising sun. In fact, the moon becomes a guide to other realms and a source of both inspiration and beauty.

A western kitchen is also favorable for you. It tends to settle your energy in the evening so that you can sink quickly into your watery realm at night.

If your kitchen gets a lot of daylight, either from the east or the south, temper it with opaque pull shades or thick blinds that allow you to shut out the light when you don't want it. Be certain you have a cozy resting spot where you can curl up with a book or your journal somewhere on the north side of the house.

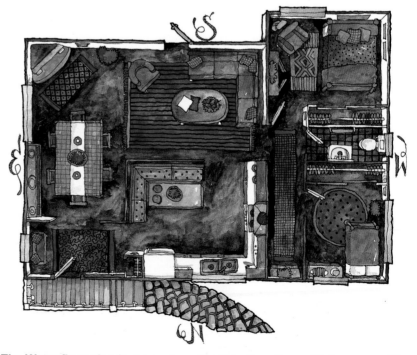

The Water floor plan is more closed in than the others. Water energy likes to be alone and hang out in small, womb-like spaces. The kitchen is in the North and features a built-in bench with a breakfast nook, a convenient place to curl up with a cup of tea in the middle of the night.

Water energy represents alignment with your deepest self. The Buddha above, sitting silently on a foundation of rock, symbolizes both the link to spiritual self (the Buddha) and the desire to stay grounded in daily reality (the rock).

How Water interacts with other elements

Water provides the depth and vision for the other four elements. Without the inner assurance and spiritual guidance of Water, we would not have any means for deciding which opinions, actions, or thoughts were personally valid. Water reminds the other elements of the big picture, encouraging ethical behavior and unblinking honesty. As much as the other elements need Water's vision, they often chaff at its need for personal integrity and try to hurry its periods of quiet introspection and stillness.

If you're trying to figure out a way to get more Water in your day, try the 3,000 year-old ritual of having tea. Tea settles the body, quiets the mind, and allows Water's presence to be felt more easily.

Water with Wood—

After the period of watery wondering, Wood naturally takes over to put Water's ideas into action. Water needs Wood to bring its ethereal concepts to life and Wood needs Water's ideas. In fact, the originating force of all ideas that align the body with the soul's purpose is Water. If Wood shuts Water out of its life, then its actions tend toward busywork, lacking a deeper sense of purpose.

Bamboo lifts energy upward, creating a rising chi characteristic of the Wood element.

These downward hanging lights and the downward movement of the staircase lend a Water quality to an otherwise Wood energy space.

The reflective quality of the granite countertop increases Water energy.

Water with Fire—

Water works its wonders slowly, much to the dismay of Fire, who would rather burn out in a brilliant instantaneous flash. In fact, Water just seems to dampen Fire's enthusiasm in all sorts of ways. Water can pull all the drama out of any event and tends to retreat when Fire wants to come out and play. Fire often thinks Water is no fun at all, yet, on some level, Fire acknowledges that it needs Water's depth to create meaning for its own displays of glory.

Leaving a teapot full of water on the stove is a sure way to dampen Fire. Be certain to pour out remaining water after the pot has boiled.

Water with Fire can be a volatile combination. In the photograph above we see a steamer drawer (a Water element) next to a gas stove (a strong Fire energy element). In the constructive cycle of the elements, Water will only put out Fire if Wood is weak. The owner of this kitchen chose to balance these energies by placing a large vase with bamboo (a strong Wood element) between the Fire and Water elements.

To bring Water into an Earth home, choose ceramic salt-and-pepper shakers with a wave pattern.

Water with Earth—

Formless, Water looks to Earth to hold it and give it shape. Without Earth, Water will continue to flow into nothingness. Only Earth's ability to confine and hold allows Water energy to pool. But Water takes its toll on Earth. As Earth gives its essence to contain the pooling Water, it loosens, and too much Water can turn stable Earth into slippery, slimy mud. Thus Water's tendency to float in a cosmic spiritual realm requires the practical, "down to earth" nature of a caretaker to meet the body's physical needs. Without Earth around to take care of them, Water people can forget to eat, dump the dishes in the sink for days, not leave the house for weeks, and generally retreat from life on the planet.

Black granite countertops are a wonderful mix of Water and Earth. The granite is strong and stable like a mountain (Earth quality). The black color and reflective nature of the granite allows energy to pool (Water quality).

This kitchen office is ideal for a Metal person who needs Water's calming depths. Although the owner chose a metal chair and organizing compartments that keep papers out of sight (a strong Metal tendency), she also chose a black "watery" desk that catches the light like a moon-lit pool.

Water with Metal–

Metal's tendency toward order and structure naturally increases Water's strength. In fact, Water needs Metal's rigor and focus to penetrate its depths and open its inner secrets. On the other hand, Metal needs Water's ability to connect to the cosmic realm in order to access the highest forms of structure and order that exist. Without Water's commitment to ethics, Metal's efforts to regulate and enforce rules have no value.

Water's gift

Water's gift to Metal is stillness. If you feel frantic and stressed at times, add a little Water to the room by increasing black or using a reflective surface.

Water with Water–

Like two nymphs, Water with Water will continue to sink deeper into the cosmic soup, possibly never to return to the Earth realm. If you've ever sat and listened to two philosophers debate the existence of God, you know what I mean. The conversation seems unending, as both people are pulled into more complex abstractions. If there's no one else in the room to bring them back to earth, and earth time, the conversation can continue indefinitely.

Water rituals

Rituals that include water, such as tea ceremonies, can be a powerful daily practice to allow Water's insights into your life.

Couple your tea ceremony with a short prayer or mantra of thanksgiving and gratitude and notice how the quality of the day improves.

Blessing water. To prepare a special dinner and bless both the food and the people who eat it, bless the water you cook with. Water is easily charged and can carry vibration into food. Use a clear glass container for this ritual. Fill the glass vase or container ⅔ full and hold your hands over the water, palms down. Speak your intended blessings out loud over the water and visualize the energy from your hands charging the water, energizing it with the same emotional quality that you hold at that moment in your heart. Use this water in cooking your meal, knowing that the food will hold the vibrational quality of your intention.

Warming your body with a hot drink will disperse excessive Water.

When Water gets excessive

Your Water is excessive when you find yourself unable to join in activities with others even when you want to, or if you're unable to move your creative ideas into action. In the body, excessive Water shows up as feeling cold and craving salty foods and you may find yourself sleeping more than normal. Dispersing excessive Water is slow going and needs time.

Force yourself to use the stove. Boil water, open a can of soup, or throw a potato in the oven.

Eat warming or spicy foods. These generate heat in the body and will help "dry up" some of your excessive Water chi.

Open blinds and pull back drapes. Find a way to let in light. If not daylight, turn on more indoor lights than normal.

Replace cool colors with warm tones. You might need to start small here, since you won't be drawn to bright colors.

Light candles. Since you tend to be drawn to dim space, light candles to bring more Fire energy into your internal world.

Keep a journal. Begin a practice of journaling whenever you catch yourself daydreaming.

Water quality

The quality of your water affects every process within your body. It doesn't take much to add a purifier to your tap or a filter to your water pitcher. And, more than any other substance, water is the most receptive to blessings. Simply saying a prayer or mantra over a bowl of water has been proven to change the molecular structure of the water. Yelling or saying angry words over the same bowl of water will make it lose its crystalline structure.

You are not a human being having a spiritual experience. You are a spiritual being having a human experience.
Dr. Wayne W. Dyer

What to include—your personal sanctuary

Your kitchen is less a place for cooking than it is for communing with spirit guides. Don't be surprised if you find you have more books in your kitchen than food, or if your favorite activity is sitting at the kitchen table staring off into space. But your Water can also benefit by consciously creating surroundings that make it easier for you to travel from the external world to your inner world, and back again. The ideas below will help you know how to ease your passage.

Let it all hang down. Cascading plants and hanging items support a Water energy vibration. They move energy lower in the body, allowing you to relax and let go of stress or anxiety.

Let stillness reign. As a place of refuge, your kitchen should be a quiet peaceful place. Remove microwaves, noisy fans, and electronic devices. Bring items which relax you into the kitchen.

Get your feet up off the floor. Add a footstool or ottoman for your couch, or put your feet up on a neighboring chair. If you get your feet off the floor, it creates a sensation of floating and prevents you from giving into Wood's desire to jump up and get things done. If you have access to the outdoors, try hanging a sky chair on the patio. Not only will your feet be off the floor, but you'll swing back and forth, and make your Water very happy.

Keep things trouble-free. China dishes, crystal goblets, and shiny pans seem trivial and require upkeep. Make your kitchen as effortless as possible. Buy stick-free pans and hire a cleaning service.

Get comfy. This is Earth energy supporting your Water. If you're going to daydream anyway, you might as well be comfortable. Plus, you'll find that Earth sofa or cushy chair will help you trust your own process more. When your physical body is supported, your spirit can soar.

Your kitchen can become an altar without looking like it was built in the 1800s. This simple altar includes a comfortable built-in bench for relaxing and slowing down. The tiny tea lights give the area a sacred quiet energy.

Keep it small and snug. Water seeks a womb, a small dark space in which ideas can gestate. Dimmer lights, cozy seating areas, and darker wall colors will all help Water energy hold itself in and not feel dispersed and scattered. Large spaces increase a feeling of vulnerability; Water begins to lose its shape and, with time, its depth.

Let your mind float. A bowl of water provides a helpful centerpiece for you to reflect and let go. Even better if the bowl is a dark blue or black color, so that the water has the illusion of depth.

Remove the clock. You do not operate on worldly time. Your best insights and contributions may come long after the clock signals that it's time to go to bed. However, if you find your Water's energy excessive, and you're too much in another world, place a clock within your view to anchor you.

Incorporate open, flowing shapes. Along with circles, add open flowing shapes such as a kidney-shaped island or a set of canisters arranged from highest to lowest. Terraces, cascading shapes, and curvy lines will increase Water energy.

Let others do the cooking. You probably don't have much enthusiasm for food preparation, maybe boiling water for tea, but that's about it. It's not a time issue for you as much as you're just not that interested in food. Feel free to leave your cupboards empty, or turn your walk-in pantry into a meditation room for one. And be certain you know a good take-out restaurant.

Organize your chaos. You might find you use your kitchen table more for sorting through piles of papers than for eating. Indeed, things might get so stacked that you can't see underneath. If so, use bins or baskets to keep your papers under control. Get a large ceramic vase for your pens and pencils. Or buy a bound journal instead of writing your ideas down on separate scraps of paper. Again, you'll find using Earth's containers and Metal's organizing skills can go a long way toward making your Water life easier.

This stained-glass window brings the flowing wavy movements of Water into the room.

Use circles

A Metal shape—circles are the most ancient symbol of continuity and continuation. They represent the death and rebirth of all life. A complete shape, the circle constantly suggests that a Water phase, death of the old and the emergence of the new, is eminent. As soon as one cycle is completed (the end of Metal), a new one is forming (the beginning of Water). Circles remind the subconscious that the Water phase (associated with the void, chaos, and a fear of death) is part of the whole and cannot be passed over. The half-round shape of this light fixture brings a Metal quality to any space suffering from too much Water.

Remodels that revive

One way I explain feng shui to first-timers is to ask if they've ever remodeled. Anyone who's remodeled remember how chaotic life gets when the chi flow is disrupted, and how good it feels to get everything back in order again. Only then can life return to normal. This is especially true of the kitchen.

A kitchen remodel can be a fast path to disaster if feng shui concepts are ignored. On the other hand, remodeling the kitchen is a powerful and effective way to remodel (or redesign) your life.

What you choose to emphasize, where you put your energy, how open or closed your space is, will all make a difference in how you live. When thinking about a kitchen remodel, think just as much about what you want in your life as what you want in your home. As you make your choices, remember that every physical change creates emotional, psychological, and spiritual shifts.

This remodeled kitchen is a tribute to healthy living. With herb gardens lining the windows, controllable sunlight, and healthy thriving plants, the owners created a kitchen that guests truly want to live in. Prep areas are close to eating areas, which allows guests to participate in the cooking. In fact, cooking becomes a part of the socializing here.

Twelve-point remodeling checklist

- ✔ Protect your back.

- ✔ Widen your passageways.

- ✔ Position the stove first, then the fridge and sink.

- ✔ Give yourself a pleasant view from the sink.

- ✔ Use the kitchen to open up the center of the home.

- ✔ Avoid vaulted ceilings with layers of crisscrossing beams.

- ✔ Design a seamless interface between old and new.

- ✔ Maintain the integrity of the structure.

- ✔ Balance the ba gua.

- ✔ Link heaven and earth.

- ✔ Put paint to work for you.

- ✔ Support your core element.

The owners of this kitchen rescued a transom window and trimwork from a demolition site to bring a 1902 quality to their new kitchen addition.

Interweave old & new

Your home is not an isolated entity floating in space. It is an integral part of an ecosystem every bit as fragile as the Brazilian rainforest. Everyone has seen the remodel that catapulted one house ten feet above every other house on the block, throwing both old and new out of integrity with each other. Likewise, we've all seen additions that look like someone tacked a "pre-fab" shed onto the back of the house. The feng shui remodel designs a seamless interface between old and new, so that each can energize and support the other.

Decide which features you love in your home, the things that drew you there in the first place, and use these features to welcome in the new. For example, if your beach-side home has white cedar shingles on the main body of the house, incorporate those same shingles into the remodeled section. Match window shapes and trim styles. Save original doors and windows from one area to use in another. Add columns to the new rear porch that match the columns on the front. You're doing more than matching architectural styles, you're energetically integrating the house. If the new space looks separate, the two spaces will pull apart. When this happens, you might find yourself living only in the new part of the house, or you might find that those family members whose rooms are in the more isolated section feel cut off from family activities.

Maintain structural integrity

To have integrity, a structure must have inherent balance, a moderate flow of energy (not too fast, not too slow), and a sense of completion in the shape. To discover what creates inherent balance, feng shui masters looked to nature. Nature, they believed, knew how to restore balance. They studied those places in nature where life thrived. Where did the grass grow green and lush? Where were the birds and animals plentiful? What consistent patterns existed in these areas and how could they create those patterns in human dwellings? They discovered that dwellings that emulated nature's patterns supported an abundant harmonious life, whereas dwellings that ignored nature's lessons created disaster. Aim to complete shapes that can be found in nature.

> **The pattern: Integrate new additions with existing features to reduce splintering chi.**

The remodels above and below might have added space, but the structures now lack integrity. When planning a remodel, design add-ons that enhance rather than detract from the original shape of the house.

Although this is a gorgeous view, the slider door exposes the kitchen to a sharp drop-off and deep gully. When planning a remodel, be certain to guard your back.

Front boundaries

If your kitchen is in the front of the house, avoid any high front boundaries. Nothing generates a more stagnant, claustrophobic energy than a high strong wall in front of you. We naturally project our energy out in the front. If you place a tall fence or wall in the front of your house, rather than behind, you're restricting yourself and you will most likely feel hemmed in and blocked, not protected.

Place the mountain at your back

The cardinal feng shui rule is to create safety and security at your back. Kitchen remodels sometimes "open up" the back of the house to connect the house with the outdoors, but open is not always ideal. Backyard views should be views of nature, not neighboring houses. If your neighbors have a view of your back (the ability to see into the back of your house), you will always feel exposed, vulnerable, and edgy.

If you don't naturally have a mountain behind you, create your own mountain. Install a tall fence, plant fast-growing trees, start a vine trellis, or build a stucco pony wall. In addition to a wall, add large boulders or large potted plants to solidify and anchor the energy at your back. Choose natural colors, both for your rocks and for your addition, that can visually become part of the ground and, thereby, become part of the stable energy of Earth. Avoid reflective surfaces when anchoring objects, since refracting light generates movement and reduces stability.

> The pattern: The more open your home is in the back, the more substantial (grounded, anchored) your back boundary should be.

This dining room was exposed and allowed the neighbors to see into the house. To create more privacy, the feng shui consultant placed a lattice-work screen in the deck area. The dining room is still connected to the outdoors, but now provides the necessary privacy.

The newly remodeled house to the right detracts rather than adds to the chi of the neighborhood. Remodels must maintain integrity, not just within their own structure, but within the structural blueprint of the entire neighborhood as well.

Maintain neighborhood integrity

The new structure of the house should enhance, rather than detract from the surrounding houses. Having the biggest, newest house on the block is not always a good thing. If your house is too far removed from the energy (look and feel) of the neighboring houses, you disrupt the energy flow of the entire neighborhood. Then, it becomes a matter of you against the rest of the neighborhood, and it takes a tremendous amount of energy on a daily basis to maintain your "position." It's sometimes a fine line between attracting chi and attracting envy. Stay in integrity with your neighbors. It will pay back tenfold.

> **The pattern: Harmonize with neighboring homes, avoid fighting chi.**

Don't measure a kitchen by its amenities

A well-designed kitchen does not have to include granite countertops, high-end appliances, or European tile. The best kitchens are those that create a secure central place for family to gather and share their days and support each other's dreams.

The kitchen below was changed by removing the wall running between the kitchen and dining room. The result shown above, opened up the center of the entire house.

Open the center

The best way to create moderate chi flow is to keep pathways open from side to side and from front to back. Remove walls, cut in windows, whatever it takes to open up the center. If the kitchen is in the center of the house, be aware of the placement of hot or cold elements such as the stove or refrigerator. The stove, microwave, and oven are the strongest yang forces in the home, these items build Fire chi and increase movement, change, and heat. Too much Fire chi can manifest in a volatile temperament or scattered thinking. Keep strong yang forces out of the center of the kitchen.

> The pattern: An open center allows chi to move side-to-side and back-to-front.

The refrigerator and sink use cold temperatures or downward-flowing water, generating strong yin forces. Yin slows the body down, lowers energy levels, and pulls your attention inward. Too much yin, and things stop. To avoid frequent colds, moodiness, or the inability to make decisions, avoid yin forces in the center.

Mixture of both

When you have both strong yang and strong yin items in the center of your kitchen or your entire home, transitions become harsh. First one way, then another, it's easy to lose your ability to moderate life's ups and downs.

> The pattern: A balanced flow of chi enhances communication and health.

The task of the center of the house is to balance the entire home, so intensely yin or yang items here disrupt the center's ability to balance everything else. If the center is out of whack, you'll feel the effects in every room of the house.

Strong yang items:

- stove
- microwave
- steamer drawers

Strong yin items:

- sink
- refrigerator
- freezer

With the strong yin energy of the sink right next to the strong yang energy of the stove, this kitchen's chi was volatile. By opening up an interior window above the sink and allowing the yin chi to move into the dining room, the energy of the entire kitchen was altered.

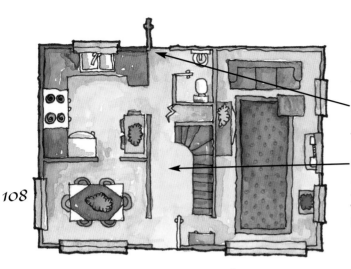

The floor plan to the left was already a rectangle, so the addition shown below was planned to enhance the Abundance area without creating missing sectors.

Since the back door, along with the bathroom, was in External Recognition, the owners wanted to slow the flow of chi by creating a new rear entrance.

Because the staircase and entrance hall are located in Health, the owners needed to keep the entrance hall as open as possible. Since this was also a bearing wall, they decided to extend the kitchen out in the back, instead of reducing the size of the hallway.

Balance the ba gua

Use your remodel to position your kitchen in an optimal place in the ba gua. As discussed earlier, the ba gua is a template for balancing the flow of chi in various aspects of your life. When remodeling, it's important to remember that if the physical structure you create lacks integrity, that lack will show up in your life. Therefore, if you create a ba gua shape that's missing the Abundance area, this lack of abundance will manifest in your pocketbook as well. Let's look at some examples of incomplete ba guas, and then show you how to adjust those same floor plans to create ba gua shapes that bring balance and wholeness.

> The pattern: Use the ba gua map as a guide to creating shapes that enhance harmony and reduce distorted chi flow.

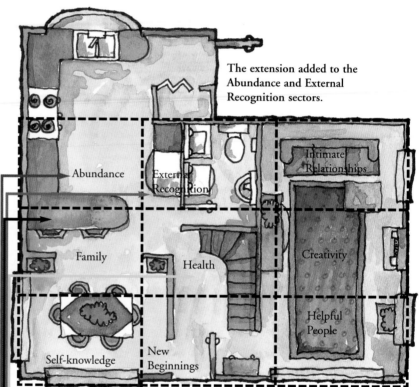

The extension added to the Abundance and External Recognition sectors.

Thousands of dollars and six months later, the owners have a house that supports how they live. The Abundance area was dramatically enhanced.

The awkward kitchen eating area was replaced by a built-in bar for two, allowing chi to flow smoothly throughout the kitchen.

The Health area was enhanced by creating a passageway for chi to move easily into the kitchen. As the chi flows in, it encounters the rounded bar, which pushes it toward the main cooking area.

The expanded bathroom shortened the hallway and prevents chi from rushing from the front of the house to the back.

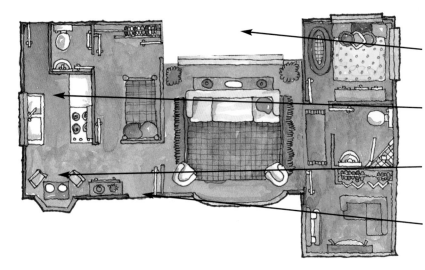

This original layout reveals a missing area in the External Recognition and Intimate Relationships sectors.

The original narrow kitchen in the Abundance area made everyone feel cramped.

The only eating area is small. This remodel needed formal and informal eating areas out of the chi flow.

The entrance is small. The couple wanted to open up new career possibilities and have a view into the house.

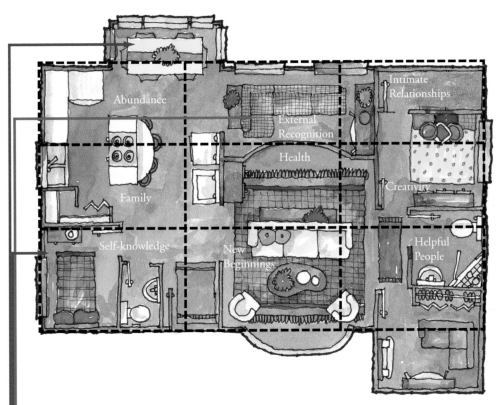

The remodel created a projection in the Abundance area and relocated the bathroom to the Journey sector. The stove is in an island, giving the cook a commanding view. With the addition of a new bar, their kitchen has become the social center of the house.

The small bedroom is perfect for the Self-knowledge area. Repositioning this bedroom and the accompanying bathroom made the remodel's open floor plan possible.

Now the External Recognition area holds a media center with stereos and televisions. The archway between the family room and the living room imitates the curve of the front window. The large picture window was replaced by two smaller windows that hold in the chi and capture strategic backyard views.

Before the remodel, the kitchen was completely separate from the rest of the house. The doorway provided only a narrow view into the next room, and the dining room was an isolated, dark hole.

By tearing down the dividing wall and uniting dining room with kitchen, the remodel placed the chef in the command position, allowed for more pleasant interaction with guests, and turned the unused dining room into a social hot spot.

Support the stove

When cooking, the goal is to infuse the food with positive vibrant chi. Vitamins, minerals, proteins, and carbohydrates are still important; but what gives food its ability to strengthen your chi, is its chi. To enhance physical health, mental health, wealth status, and personal safety, you need to eat food with strong chi. There are two ways you can strengthen the chi in your food: (1) support the person preparing the food, thereby raising their chi, and (2) honor the position and cleanliness of the stove.

Your remodel might include some of the following adjustments:

Remove the wall between the stove and the adjoining room. By opening the view in front of the stove, you not only expand the cook's visual range, but you energetically expand the reach of the stove to the rooms beyond. If necessary, separate range burners from the oven so anyone cooking on the burners has a view of the door.

Avoid flat mirrors behind the stove. Many feng shui books advise mirroring behind the stove to give a view of the door. Although this adjustment works fine for most Chinese, Americans tend to be taller. You should never position a mirror where you can't see your entire face and six inches above your head. Additionally, it can be more startling than helpful to see yourself cooking in a large mirror.

Teapot power

If your stove is against a wall, use a rounded teapot to act as a mirror, allowing you to see behind you.

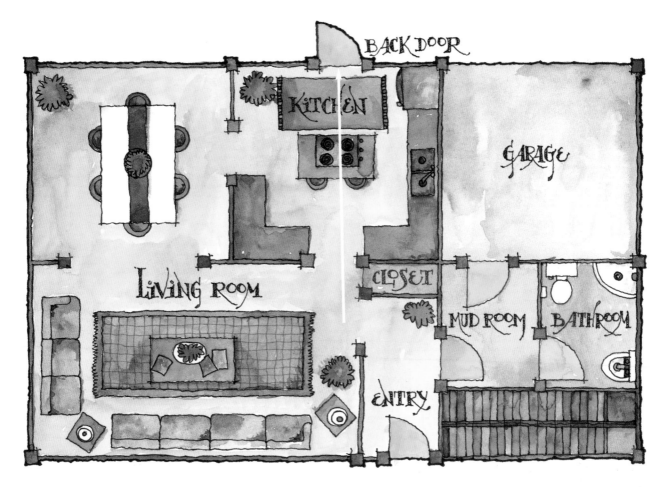

Although this stove is positioned to give the cook a view of the door, it's also right in front of the back door. In this situation, it's best to situate the stove against a wall rather than have it line up with the chi flow moving in and out of a door.

Buy the best stove you can afford. This is a tough one for people who don't cook much. The stove is the strongest wealth symbol in your home. It represents your ability to take advantage of opportunities and transform potential chi into actualities. If you find you are unable to make things happen financially or your timing seems off, invest in your stove. And remember, when you go out stove shopping, six burners are better than four because they represent more opportunities.

Avoid hanging heavy objects above the cook. Anything that weakens or threatens the cook while at the stove should be avoided. This includes heavy racks with hanging pots and pans, ceilings fans, large light fixtures, etc. Plan to position pots where they are easily accessible, but not threatening. Ceiling fans should be avoided anywhere within six feet of cooking areas, and light fixtures are best kept light and high up above the head.

Keep the stove out of the main chi flow. To figure out where the chi flow is in your kitchen, draw a line between the main doorway leading into the kitchen to any other doors leading out.

112

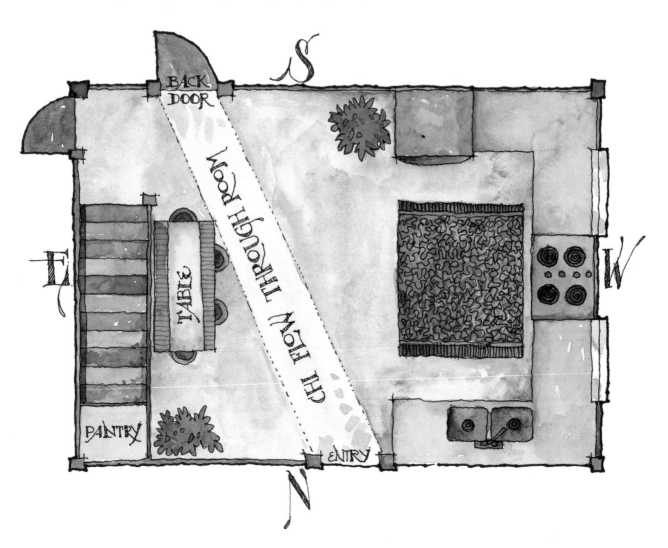

In remodeling this kitchen, Mary Dennis of Feng Shui 2000, Inc., placed the stove in the work island to give the cook a more protected position, thereby raising the cook's chi.

Place the stove in an island. This placement is the best for giving the stove a protected position with a view of the door and away from the room's main chi flow. Use the island to buffer and protect the cook and consider a two-level island that allows the cook's realm to be separate from the island's eating area.

Set up the stove according to who does the cooking. It should be easy for the cook to reach the back burners, since using all four burners represents taking advantage of all of life's opportunities. If two people share the kitchen equally, make certain each feels their personal tastes and needs have been addressed.

Activate your stove

Make an offering to the universe to express your gratitude for all that you have received. Replace your burner knobs with bright red ones (the color red activates chi) or use a copper teakettle (copper is the most yang metal).

Vaulted ceilings

Vaulted ceilings may seem like a good idea, but a vaulted ceiling (symbolic of Heaven's influence) can dwarf the human principle, making you and your children feel small and inadequate. To bring the human factor back into proportion, create a false ceiling.

Link heaven & earth

A vaulted or two-story ceiling can rob a kitchen of its nurturing supportive chi. Because we use ceilings to ground ourselves and stabilize our movements, a vaulted ceiling removes this stabilizing influence. When the ceiling is too far from the floor, the human principle is dwarfed and heaven's guidance feels far away. In

The pattern: If the real ceiling is too high, create a false ceiling to bring your eye, and your chi, back down.

this case, create a false ceiling about eight feet high. You can generate this effect by hanging three light fixtures in a row or by placing your pictures so that they form a horizontal line. The goal is to stop the eye at normal ceiling height.

114

Hanging pictures on the horizontal instead of the vertical stabilizes the chi and stops upward movement.

This built-in seating area balances the open wall of windows, creating a space to relax and snuggle up.

Build walls that hold you

The basic reason we live in houses is protection. Walls should hold our energy in and keep other things out. The thicker the walls, the greater the sense of comfort and safety. If your design includes walls of glass windows, you might lose this basic sense of safety and comfort. We usually plan window walls to take advantage of a stunning view, but remember to balance this openness with an equal amount of enclosure. Balance a wall of windows, with an enclosed sitting area. Place an L-shaped sofa in the room, so that you can snuggle up in the corner of the sofa, relax, and enjoy the view without being drained by it. Other ideas include framing a smaller window in a wall of glass block, keeping the light, but not losing the chi. Plants in front of the window wall will recirculate the chi back into the room. Nooks, niches, and cupboards can balance an open wall of windows. Anchor your windows with cabinetry on both sides.

> **The pattern: Whenever you create an open interface with the outside, create interior enclosures to hold the chi.**

Solid walls

Create the illusion of thick solid walls with:

- **the appearance of stone or adobe walls, using a mottled paint technique.**

- **built-in nooks.**

- **archways and curved interior windows.**

- **an exposed brick wall. If you don't have a brick wall to expose, lay one on top of your existing wall.**

- **crown molding and thick window trim.**

Pleasing views

Give yourself a pleasant view when cooking. What you see influences your mood. In fact, an unpleasant view can influence your chi even more than standing with your back to your door.

Move your stove into an island rather than placing it against a wall. If you feel it's best placed against the wall, or if size restraints prevent an island, give yourself a pleasant view by hanging a picture behind the stove. Fresh fruits, flowers, and still-life paintings are best here.

Above all, make certain you're not looking out a door when standing at your stove, or it will be difficult to pull your chi in and transfer it to the food.

The owners made the following changes to their home to combine the chi of the dining room and the kitchen:
cut out an interior window
removed the door between the kitchen and dining room
added a false transom window above the doorway

Physically connect the kitchen

A common trend is the extension of the kitchen into the family area. Kitchens have long represented the central source of nourishment and grounding. When the kitchen is cut off from other areas of the house, that nourishment is cut off as well. There are many ways to connect your kitchen to other areas of your home.

Remove a wall. If you can give up the counter/wall space between your kitchen and dining room, this will dramatically change the flow of chi throughout the space. If you need separation some of the time, install sliding Tatami screens where the wall used to be.

Add an interior window. Cut a window into the wall between the kitchen and the social rooms. When placing a window, stand in the kitchen and imagine what you'll see once the window is there. Pick your best view from the kitchen side. Be certain to make the window higher than your countertops, so you can see out, but guests can't see messy counters.

Transform doors into passageways. Take a door off and frame it so it appears to be a passageway. Doors hold the ability to close off one part of yourself from another, passageways encourage openness.

Use paint, walls, and flooring choices. Link rooms together through color and flooring. Paint the trim or walls the same color or use the same flooring to visually unify the rooms. Get creative. Perhaps the warm white you use for trim in your kitchen becomes the wall color in your adjoining living room.

Perhaps you'll use cork as a backsplash in the kitchen and then on the floor in the adjoining laundry area.

You can visually link this existing dining room to a remodeled kitchen by using the same grapevine stencil in both the kitchen and dining room.

Architectural integrity

Match architectural remnants or trimwork. If you can't change the structure of your house, you can join the energy of the kitchen to other parts of the house by linking. This feng shui adjustment relies on the fact that you carry what your eye just saw in one room into the next. If the rooms are similar enough, the eye tells the mind that the two rooms are part of one larger space. Match the trim of your living room with that in your kitchen. If the front of the house uses delicate finials, link that area to your kitchen by installing the same finials above the kitchen door.

Link your kitchen to other rooms in the house by using similar objects, such as these copper pots. Use intention and focused mental energy to link the copper pot to the copper urn. Once fused, the items will bridge energy indefinitely.

Energetically connect the kitchen

Link the kitchen to the rest of the home using symbols. Energy moves where directed. Like water in a stream, it will follow the routed course unless a force alters that course. That force can be your intention, and you can anchor your intention by strategically placing symbolic objects or symbols in your home. To use symbols to link your kitchen to other areas of the home, find more than one representation of the same symbol. For example, you might select candles to represent warmth and compassion. First, place the largest of the symbols, in this case candles, in the kitchen. Then walk to the other rooms and place the other candles, imagining as you do so that the energy of the first candle is connected, as if by a stream of light, to each candle that you place. Choose your symbols carefully; what you choose to symbolically unite your home will affect the overall feeling there.

> The pattern: Link rooms energetically using symbols and tokens to increase chi flow and communication between those rooms.

Create order so energy can flow. Organizing a drawer, a cupboard, or even a closet will radically alter how energy flows through your kitchen. If you've even got 15 minutes, set a timer and tell yourself that until that timer goes off you are going to tackle the silverware drawer (or whatever drawer is calling to you). You'll be amazed at the transformation 15 minutes of organizing a day can achieve.

One of my favorite chi raisers is a glass frame filled with a friend's wild-flowers pressed between the glass.

Power of ritual

A morning coffee chat with your partner, a family hug, or a weekly calendar planning, honors the emotional connection that may occur in a kitchen.

Consider adding some of the following rituals to your kitchen environment:

- **Sharing the day's events while preparing dinner.**

- **Daily spelling bees for your youngster.**

- **Personal quiet time for journaling or a cup of tea.**

- **Music with dinner to expand your family's awareness of different cultures and styles.**

- **Storytelling at dinner.**

- **Dream-sharing over a family breakfast.**

- **Taking turns preparing a favorite meal.**

Harvest the positive chi from your childhood by incorporating your favorite family traditions into your daily routine. Such regular rituals will enhance your relationship with family and with your kitchen and you will want to take better care of it.

Chi raisers

Not all of us can remodel our kitchens, but you can always raise the chi by adding a small object that lifts your spirits and makes you smile. "Chi raisers" are objects that remind you of a wonderful life memory or capture the essence of how you choose to live your life. Chi raisers can be simple and not cost a thing. My favorite chi raiser is a note my son wrote that appeared one day out of the blue, taped to the refrigerator door, "Be Grateful." Following suit, I wrote another one and taped to the wall next to my sitting chair. It said, "Be Amazed." Find what pleases you, delights you, and makes you feel alive, and use these objects to tease yourself into engaging fully in whatever lies before you each day.

> **The pattern: Use chi raisers to remind you of life's most beautiful moments.**

Little adjustments can make a difference in how your kitchen looks and feels. Cover up unsightly cords and plugs by using a picture, a plant, or a basket.

Eliminate fighting chi

Many modern structures seem to live by the motto that the more visually intersecting lines, slicing and dicing through the air, the better. Not so in the feng shui remodel. A ceiling full of intersecting or crossing beams and slanted ceilings with sharp angular "architectural features" does nothing more than disrupt the chi. Because energy will follow one line, and then the other, whenever you see two beams or two

> **The pattern: Crisscrossing layers over your head result in crossed signals of all kinds. Avoid miscommunication by eliminating one of the layers.**

angles coming together, the energy that travels on those beams (or walls) will cross as well. Every structure, like a beam, has an energy shaft that travels along the beam. Energy shafts don't just cross over each other in a harmonious fashion. Like irritable children, they fight whenever they get close. Even if your beams or lines don't physically connect, different angles and views draw them together in your mind's eye, and the fighting chi is visually present nonetheless. Layers of crisscrossing beams are a sure sign that the people in the home will have a hard time getting along.

Paint one layer of beams the same color as the ceiling. This will visually eliminate a layer helping your eye separate them.

Take out a layer. Often you can lower your ceiling enough to eliminate one layer of beams. If you can get down to one layer of beams, or reduce the amount of intersecting angles, you eliminate much of the fighting chi.

Use color to bring the ceiling down below the lowest level of intersecting beams. The ceiling does not have to be flat. If there are four feet of crisscrossing beams and angles, paint the ceiling, beams, intersecting angles, everything a darker color than your walls down to the lowest beam. The angles and beams visually merge together and flatten out, and the fighting chi decreases dramatically.

When you can't remove the beams overhead, add grounding elements below. This planter box pictured above strengthens Earth energy and alleviates the oppressive chi of crisscrossing overhead beams.

Remodeling is more than adding—it is making your space work for you. This means any remodeling plan should begin with a life accessment.

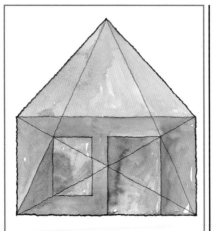

Positioning openings

Windows and doorways need to be positioned according to the pitch of the roof and the overall size of the house. To see how your windows and doors line up, draw a star through a frontal view of your house (as shown above). The primary windows and doors should line up on the star's intersecting lines.

Take advantage of framing

Once windows, walls, and doorways are framed in, but before they're built, reevaluate your views. Things are different when built than they looked on paper. It's hard to know exactly what your view will capture or how the chi will flow until the building is framed.

Reevaluate window size. A west window might seem like a good idea, but you might find it lets in views of your neighbor's roof, which is in need of reroofing. At this stage, you can still make changes. You could keep the window and change the size, or possibly use a smaller window

> The pattern: Use the energizing and mood-altering effects of sunlight to raise the chi.

with glass block surrounding it. Either way you won't end up staring at a mess every day, wishing that lightening would strike the neighbor's house so that they have to put on a new roof.

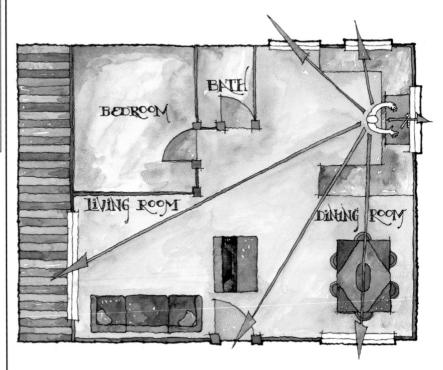

When framing windows, assess your views from the kitchen. Open as many lines of sight as possible. This floor plan allows for a view out the dining room window, a view of the front door, a view out the sliding door from the living room, and views out of three kitchen windows, all while standing at the kitchen sink.

This kitchen looks out onto a backyard gazebo set up to take full advantage of warm summer nights.

Create a balanced view. This doesn't necessarily mean symmetrical, but often moving a window a few inches left or right can frame an outside view in a more balanced way. Your view should have the same amount of "visual weight" on both sides. If there's a large interesting tree on one side of your view and nothing but grass on the other, either move the tree to the middle of the view (by moving your window) or expand the view so that you bring something of visual interest in on the empty side.

Watch doorways. Be certain nothing blocks your entrance or exit from your house. Once the framing is done, you may realize that, if you left the back doorway where you thought it should go, a large tree would block your pathway. It's easier to move that doorway now, than be faced with the prospect of cutting down the tree later.

Bring in filtered light

Filtered light is achieved with inset panes, sheer curtains, or leaves against the panes. The filter softens a harsh sun and creates the impression of depth, which increases the comforting Earth energy in the room.

Dead space

If your kitchen is located in the center of your home and has no outside windows, bring in light from the ceiling. This could take the form of a skylight or, if the distance to the roof is great, a sky tunnel. Often called solar tubes, these sky tunnels can bring natural light in through virtually any roof system.

Plan for light

Sunlight is one of the most powerful, positive forces in the kitchen. It can break up stagnant chi, warm a yin space, and energize a dark corner. In your present kitchen, does sunlight flood through the window above the sink? Does sunlight warm spots on the floor? Does sunlight dance on your table or countertops? Be aware that wherever the light rests, the place is transformed.

Choose window treatments carefully. The same sun can be comforting one moment and blasting the next. The right window treatments allow you to benefit from, but not be bullied by, the sun. There are options available now that make it possible to do just about anything. If the western sun shines a little too brightly in the evening, use a transparent shade that allows in the entire view while cutting the glare. Many companies now carry shades that allow you to put the top down or bring the bottom up, depending on the location of the sun.

Find your stunning views and use your remodel to open up your kitchen to the great outdoors.

Allow bulbs, plant starts, and seasonal flowers to enjoy direct sunlight while bringing life into the kitchen.

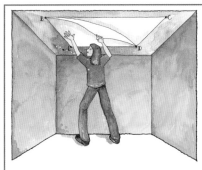

Sealing a skylight or window

Installing a new skylight or window in your kitchen requires cutting an opening. Energetically, this process is similar to performing surgery on the body. Whenever you cut an opening into an existing structure, it's wise to seal the cut. The following method for sealing a skylight or window is both simple and effective.

Rub your hands together to get the blood flowing to this part of your body. Using the flat palm of your hand, connect to the chi of the existing structure. Keep moving over this area until your palm begins to tingle. Using this tingling energy, move your palm over the area, starting in one corner and working across the area, as if you were painting. Again using the flat palm of your hand, go around the circumference, smoothing out rough edges.

Let's say your kitchen is located in the Helpful People sector of the ba gua. Helpful People is the energy pattern associated with community building, sharing, and connecting spiritually, and relationships with mentors and benefactors. You might not notice any differences at first. But the more you shut down and disconnect from this energy pattern in your space, the harder it will be to sustain a flow of energy to this part of your life. You might notice that communication between colleagues or your boss seems more distant; perhaps you don't feel the same sense of "connection" that you felt before. Perhaps it's God that feels more distant, or perhaps your neighbors suddenly decide to install a six-foot fence between your property line and theirs.

How shifts in energy ripple out vary considerably, but 3–6 months is a key time frame. If you can get your project done within three months and are happy with the results, most relationships can weather the disconnect. If a project drags on for more than six months, most relationships will feel the strain.

Project junkie

The tendency to stack one project on top of another magnifies chaos. We start a second project because we feel uncomfortable in our space and want to change it. The second project brings a short-lived sense of hope and new life, because we anticipate change. When the second project remains unfinished, the energetic weight of the new project falls upon the first, and becomes an even stronger energy drain. The more unfinished projects we have, the more drained we are, and the less likely we have the energy, enthusiasm, or money to finish them.

Decide which project would bring you the most pleasure, and focus all your energy on completing that project. Project junkies have a hard time enjoying the fruits of their labors. It does not hold the same rush for them to finish something as it does to start something. Give yourself the gift of feeling complete. You'll notice you have more energy for other projects and you'll feel less compulsion to constantly start something new.

Be certain a remodel doesn't go bad

How long it takes to complete your remodel is a key factor in determining the impact it will have on you and your life. Remodels tend to drag on and on, and can be incomplete for years. Besides being a nuisance, a chaotic space is one most people avoid. We block it out and pretend we don't see the wires sticking out of the ceiling where the lighting fixture is supposed to be. The problem is, the more you block out the influence of your surrounding environment, the more you energetically disconnect from the life aspect associated with that area. If you remain disconnected for more than 3–6 months, it's difficult not to suffer considerable strain in that part of your life.

For example, you want to remodel your kitchen. You tear down a wall, rip the faces off your cupboards and order new appliances. But the cupboards don't come in on time or the new opening doesn't get trimmed out. Maybe your carpenter takes on too many projects at once, or the company that produces those exact cupboards goes on strike. Whatever the reason, it drags on. Meanwhile, you can't stand going in your kitchen. You eat out as much as possible. You avoid looking at your physical environment because it's a constant reminder that someone else is making you wait or you have entered a deal gone bad. You disconnect. Don't allow yourself to remain disconnected from any one space for more than six months.

The clutter-free kitchen

Although people in ancient China struggled to gather enough to survive, today's kitchens typically suffer from too much stuff, rather than not enough. The professional tools designed to save us time and energy actually consume both. When you have accumulated more than you need or more than you can personally use, your kitchen is draining you instead of nourishing you.

Clutter-clearing and organizing are skills that can be taught and learned. Although the two are often lumped together, clutter-clearing is actually the first stage of getting organized. This chapter takes you through the steps for letting go of excess clutter and for organizing what's left. According to Marla Dee, a professional organizer, "Organizing is clearing and arranging your environment so that it reflects you, supports you, and conveniently provides all the tools you need in your daily life." Marla's approach deals with both clutter-clearing and organizing in one integrated system.

Only do one step at a time! Don't mix the steps. Things get messy when you start one step and then, halfway through, drop it to begin another. Before you start, promise yourself that you'll finish each step before starting the next one.

S Sort it
T Toss it
A Assign it a home
C Containerize it
K Keep it up
S Simplify it

Don't do the entire kitchen all at once. Start with a small area that feels neutral to you—a drawer or a countertop, nothing more.

128 **Before starting the organizing process, the client typically stuck items wherever they could fit.**

Here the client has pulled everything out of the cupboard and sorted it into piles. Now she knows exactly what is in the cupboard.

Here is the same cupboard after the client went through the entire STACKS process.

This above collection of plasticware is an example of like items grouped together.

Sort it

It all starts with sorting. The first thing you do is empty everything out of the area you are organizing. Group like items together: rubber bands, plastic flatware, spice packets. Don't think about whether or not you'll keep them or where you're going to put it all when you're done, it's vital that the first step of this process is decision-free. All you're doing is placing things in categories.

Prepare boxes ahead of time for your piles. If you're dealing with a large area like a pantry, your floor space might not be adequate to handle everything that comes tumbling out.

Label piles as you go. Labeling provides your brain with immediate visual recognition of the categories you're using. Don't worry about whether you know what categories you're going to need. The categories create themselves as you go. Simply label each one as you create it. Keep categories as general as possible, but choose ones that work for you. Labels don't need to be fancy. Brightly colored sticky notes work great.

Completely empty out the area you are organizing. When people get halfway through emptying a space, they're tempted to move on to the next step. Resist this temptation. One way to keep yourself from succumbing to this temptation is to dump everything on the floor or a table. That way, you won't stop halfway through.

Toss it

Now that you can see everything, decide what to keep and what to let go. Look for obsolete dates on food, rusty bakeware, and lidless containers. Get honest about what you actually use.

Take one pile at a time. Turn away from your other piles to keep yourself from getting distracted by them.

If you love the item and it lifts your energy keep it. However, it's important to distinguish between items you love and items given to you by people you love. To keep clutter down, choose one or two items that best represent the person and let the rest go.

Don't keep anything out of obligation. Honor the intention behind the gift and let the things go.

Beware of the urge to keep something, just in case. These situations involve the fear that you are not enough or that life will not provide all that you need when you need it.

Have boxes ready

- "Garbage" box for any broken, or incomplete items.

- "Charity" box for items going to shelters.

- "Used" box for items to be sold at a yard sale.

- "Giveaway" box for items to keep in the family or share with friends.

- "Gift" box for items to give away as gifts.

After you Sort, you're going to Toss. This homeowner has pulled out her garbage can and is in the process of deciding whether things stay or go.

This enclosed area keeps appliances handy while avoiding a cluttered countertop.

Place all your appliances together in one area. Since appliances usually come in unruly shapes and sizes, putting all your odd bulky things together will minimize their impact on your overall kitchen.

Assign a home

When you have sorted all the piles, what you have left are the things you want to keep. Congratulations on making conscious choices on what to store in your kitchen. It is now time to assign everything a home. This starts the organizing phase of the process.

Fill high areas first. These are items you only need once a year or on special occasions.

Keep like things together. Putting like things together saves time and increases your ability to focus.

Place items close to where you use them. There are things you use every day. You cook, you clean, you take phone messages, you pull the bib out for the baby. First, identify your daily tasks. Write them down. Now think about where you perform those tasks and place the necessary items close to that area.

This homeowner stores her spices under her stove burners. Not only do the spices strengthen the yang chi of the stove, but they're also handy and ready to use.

This pantry was completely rearranged in the following ways:
Lightweight and seldom-used items were placed on the top shelf and careful attention was given to making sure they didn't hang out over the shelf.
The most commonly used items were placed in the middle, making them easy to see and grab.
Items used by the family's young children were placed on the lower shelves so that the kids could both get and put away their playthings by themselves.

Place the most-used daily items at shoulder height. This is prime real estate, don't fill it with dog food. Also, remember who will be using the items. For example, you can create a "kids" shelf in the pantry, cupboard, or refrigerator that holds the items they need all the time.

Don't place heavy, breakable, or bulky items over your head. This creates dangerous, precarious energy and weakens your chi.

Personal mantras

Invoke any of the following as your personal mantra and reason for clearing and organizing your space.

"My environment reflects me and supports my life."

"Everybody and everything deserves a home."

"Letting go helps me grow."

"There is no pain in change."

"There is no pain in growth. There is only pain in resistance to change and resistance to growth."

"Healthy energy is moving energy."

"I am surrounded by things I use and love."

This refrigerator above serves as the family's communication center. Here children and parents track each other's schedules, keep up on chores, and leave messages.

Labels on containers and shelves are especially helpful when organizing spaces for younger children. If they can see the label, it's one less thing they have to think about. You'll be surprised what a difference it can make.

Containerizing

Once you've finished sorting and tossing, you'll know what containers you need, how many, and how big. Take the time to find the right container for the junk drawer, or stacking shelves for canned goods, or wood dividers for your silverware. Once you have the right container, putting things away becomes an aesthetically pleasing activity. Making this part of your life fun is vital in keeping up with your clutter and making organization a daily part of your life. Here are some hints on choosing appropriate containers.

Let your personality be seen and felt. Think about what you've learned in the other chapters regarding your personal energy type and choose containers that support your essence. Choosing containers you love brings more nurturing chi into your kitchen.

Create a family communication center. Although we don't often think about it, good communication requires containers. Communication containers include:

- current wall calendar
- family bulletin board
- message pad
- pens & pencils
- chalkboard
- goal charts
- personal inspiration pictures (for your communication with your subconscious)
- photos of loved ones
- magnetic poetry for the fridge

Label containers. Label areas in the pantry to develop a system and for easy retrieval. Especially if you live with other family members, getting a new system going requires educating everyone as to where things should be. You can label shelves and containers.

Tackle one drawer at a time. Here's how you would use the **STACKS** system to organize a junk drawer.

Sort: Dump the drawer upside down on the counter and get everything out. Sort the items into like piles. Put all the batteries together, group the pens and pencils, etc.

Toss: Decide what's garbage and what's worthy junk. Throw the garbage away.

Assign: Now that you know what you are going to keep, count your items to see how many containers you'll need.

Contain: Use containers you enjoy. Because this homeowner had gone through the sorting, tossing, and assigning phases, and knew what she had, she was able to purchase beautiful wood organizers that fit her belongings perfectly.

Keep it up: The end result is a junk drawer that you want to show off to your friends, rather than a chaotic mess. It's also easy to "Keep it up" because the containers do the sorting.

Simplify: Applying this process throughout the entire kitchen made it easier for this client to simplify her life on other levels as well.

Intuition

Intuition is the powerful sense of knowing whether something is right or not by connecting to a shared consciousness. This energetic force transcends time and personalities.

Many feng shui masters intentionally give students conflicting advice to help them understand the power of intuition in reading the energy of a space.

Feng shui is a series of guidelines that work to put you in touch with your intuition, not replace it.

Intuition is your permission to play. Try things out, see how they feel. Follow your intuition rather than rules. As you clean and organize your home, be certain to pay attention to how your body feels.

Keeping it up

Keeping it up is the daily care of putting items back in their places. You might need to change your belief that things will go back to the way they were before you got organized.

Work with your family, not against them. If you've organized your things into zones and labeled your categories, the job of putting things back where they belong is greatly simplified. Because upkeep is a family endeavor, it's important to involve the entire family in the organizing process as much as possible. Ask each member of the household how they would prefer to have things set up and then decide on a system that takes everyone's needs into account.

Give yourself a junk drawer. The kitchen tends to be a natural dumping ground. The countertops, top of the refrigerator, and drawers collect everything from nails to corncob holders to magnets—all those little items that just don't have a home. Honor this and give yourself a junk drawer, a nice big one, with a multicompartment insert to hold rubber bands, tacks, tape, tools, etc.

Schedule regular times to keep up your system. Most of your upkeep will be done on a daily or weekly basis. However, scheduling an annual day to sort, toss, and rework your system is a gift everyone should give themselves. Each time you go through this process, you'll find you let go of another layer of unused items, and that you get clearer about who you are and what you want from life.

Consider where new items will fit in your existing scheme. Don't bring something new in before first making a place for it.

Simplifying

Simplifying is an ongoing process. It requires honesty in looking at what you really need and use. Most of us approach clutter-clearing and simplifying in layers. We let go of what we're ready to release, and a year later, we let go of more. Honor the process.

Don't recreate clutter. Our bodies are accustomed to a certain pattern and will naturally seek to repeat it. To change the pattern we must let ourselves enjoy the freedom that comes with fewer things to care for.

Implement a three-day waiting period. Most decisions are not so crucial that they must be made this very day. Waiting a minimum of three days will carry you past the impulsive desire to accumulate triggered by your old pattern and give you more choice over what you bring home. If you don't use it within the week after bringing it home, chances are you don't need it and might not ever use it. Give yourself permission to return items that you don't use or that you can't find a place for within the first week.

Spend time in nature. We keep excessive things in order to feel grounded, safe, and connected. The more you let go of your clutter, the greater your need to find your grounding, safety, and connection in other ways. One of the most effective ways to increase all three in your life is to spend conscious time in nature. During the clearing process, and for the 27 days following this process, spend at least 10 minutes every day outside. You might not get to that hidden canyon or spend the afternoon on the sailboat, but you can at least walk outside and listen to birds, watch the clouds move, feel the sun, and touch the ground.

Say no to what you don't need. Trust that the universe can and will provide what you need when you need it.

Shopping test

Before purchasing something new, ask the following questions:

Do I love it?

Will I honestly use it?

Where will it be stored?

Will it take time, energy, and money to maintain?

Who will care for this item or implement its use?

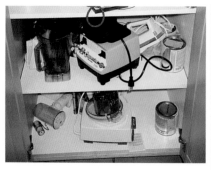

The owner of this cupboard went through the STACKS process in one hour and ended up with the organized version of the same cupboard below.

General hints for getting & staying organized

Enlist a friend. Choose someone nonjudgmental, who has your best interests in mind. Take turns, if you're both clutter bugs.

Have fun. Play music and dance or hum while you work. Dress comfortably so that you can sit on the floor for a long period of time. Play a funny movie while you sort and toss.

Calendar the event. This action is your personal vow that you will do this process no matter what excuses your mind devises.

Set aside uninterrupted time. Clutter-clearing takes a lot of courage. If you stop halfway through, it takes just as much energy to get going again. Allow twice as long as you think it will take, and do it the first time.

Use high-energy time. Organizing shouldn't be the last thing you do at the end of a long day.

A beautiful, highly efficient kitchen doesn't happen overnight. Keep working the STACKS program, area by area, until you achieve balance.

Organization process chart

	Actions	Cautions	Tricks	Rewards
Sort	Sort into piles of like with like.	Don't start making decisions yet.	Label piles to stay focused.	You will know exactly what you have.
Toss	Decide whether to keep the item or give it away.	Don't decide where to put it yet.	Tackle one pile at a time.	Your home will hold only those things that you love and use.
Assign a home	Decide where to put it.	Divide your home into activity zones.	Place your items in the associated activity zone.	Everything will be where you need it, when you need it.
Contain	Find the right amount and size of containers.	Don't forget to find containers for your papers.	Use containers that reflect your personality.	The right containers mean things stay put away.
Keep it up	Organizing is a daily practice, not a one-time event.	Give paperwork a specific time every week.	Choose a high-energy time of day for your maintenance.	Your whole life will be more "in the flow" and free of blocks.
Simplify	Don't bring in something new unless it passes "the test."	Avoid new items that require extensive upkeep.	The test: Do I love it? Will I use it? Do I have room for it?	You feel free, energized, and amazingly abundant.

Fresh fruits and vegetables contain chi that has reached a fullness of expression. That is, its energy has been transformed from a potential state into matter.

Abundance in the kitchen—
feng shui alchemy

The kitchen is one of the key areas in any home for generating financial growth. Regardless of where your kitchen falls in the ba gua, it represents your ability to generate chi and to transform potential energy into actualities. Since money is energy that has already been transformed from its potential state (an opportunity or job) into matter (the green stuff you put in the bank), the more you energize this area, the more you will enjoy all forms of abundance.

Fruits or vegetables gathered into a bowl are a strong Abundance adjustment because the bowl represents your ability to accumulate. Place your fruit bowl in the rear-left corner of your kitchen, if possible, since this area relates to Abundance. Whenever you stock your fruit bowl, visualize that your ability to gather to yourself the necessary resources is increasing. Taking a moment to visualize links your chi to the chi of the fruit bowl and increases its ability to support your energy.

This herb garden was placed right behind the sink, making it easy for the owner to water it and be energized by it.

Grow your abundance

The kitchen is a perfect place to grow herbs and vegetables. Growing plants that can actually be turned into food and digested are strong symbols for increasing your ability to take advantage of the opportunities life affords you. Any green growing plant will vitalize your space; but growing food, even if it's just a planter full of tomatoes, increases your ability to generate wealth exponentially. Whenever you water your plant, visualize that you are investing in your future and caring for your financial needs.

To invite Abundance, plant nine I Ching coins (or gold one-dollar coins) under a growing plant and place as close to the stove as is feasible. *Note: Avoid placing small pocket change under your plant, such as pennies or dimes, since these coins are typically what's handed out to beggars.*

Noncook methods

If you're adamant that cooking is not for you, resort to other forms of alchemy. In some way, on a daily basis, transform raw materials into a new creation that has the ability to nourish you on some level: financial, physical, or emotional. Here are some ideas:

- **Working out on a regular basis transforms potential chi into actual muscle.**

- **Making jewelry or a craft transforms your time and energy into a marketable product.**

- **Taking a meditation class can create inner calmness and peace.**

Moving potential chi into the realm of matter in a way that works for you is what's important here. We are creative beings and creation should be a daily activity. Think about what you would like to create in your life and find a daily way to work toward your goal.

Cooking in your kitchen is essential to generating wealth in your life. People who never cook often suffer severe financial drains, even when their financial situation seems secure. Eating out every day depletes your body's resources, your creative ability, and your pocketbook.

Use the stove

Maybe you're already using your stove and opportunities are still not as plentiful as you would like. Any of the following will raise and expand the chi of your stove, making it easier for you to draw opportunities to you.

Keep it clean. A dirty stove slows and stagnates chi.

Hang a round faceted crystal above the stove. This traditional remedy works both physically and symbolically to direct chi out in a radius of 360°, surrounding your stove. The crystal will also help balance and smooth out finances that tend to be fine one month but in trouble the next.

Light it up. A bright light above the cooking area lifts the chi and opens up your higher energy centers, making it easier for you to be creative and, therefore, profitable.

Use all four burners. Since the stove represents your connection with external opportunities, only using the front two burners is akin to answering only half your phone calls. To activate all of your potential, use all four burners.

Magnify your potential. Do not place a mirror where you will constantly view yourself with your head cut off. Buy a six burner stove or use a round reflective teapot to visually double your burners.

Make an offering to the universe. Dedicate an object on your stove as a symbol of gratitude for the blessings, opportunities, and health you currently enjoy. Regardless of your present situation, the ability to feel gratitude for your blessings is a powerful chi raiser. Find the truth and the good in your life and it will expand. Hold the object you choose for gratitude. Hold it in your hand and mentally remind yourself of all the things you feel grateful for. This imbues the object with your chi and creates powerful anchors for your thoughts and emotions.

The stove is outside energy that you use to cook your food into something you use to nurture and support yourself. When you don't use your stove, you cut yourself off from external sources of energy.

If your stove is placed on a diagonal with an empty space behind it, be certain to fill that space with spices, oils, or plants to avoid weakening the stove's chi.

The healthy kitchen

As the room most concerned with strengthening physical and mental well-being, the state of the kitchen impacts the entire house. The kitchen is also the room where volatile energies come together in close proximity and the risk of physical and psychological injury greatly increases. Cuts, burns, slipping and falling, poisonings, all happen in the kitchen. Regardless of your personal style, special care should be taken to create a place of safety and comfort in the kitchen, and reduce the risk of injury. This section contains feng shui adjustments and recommendations that will increase and strengthen chi, reduce risk, and support the human energy system.

You can improve the state of your family's health just by how you decorate your kitchen. The above kitchen is sparsely decorated and does not encourage cooking. A few adjustments (see photo left) create a more yang environment, full of color, light, and vibrant living chi. This kitchen will activate the immune system and raise the chi level of the entire house. The yang kitchen will also encourage the family to live and interact with each other in a warm friendly way.

Kitchen safety

More accidents occur in the kitchen than any other room. Walkways too close to cooking areas result in scalding, while sharp knives and electrical appliances are a common hazard. To reduce accidents review the following suggestions:

Install an island or butcher block. These additions act as buffers for the stove from the general walkway.

Place a rug parallel to the walkway. This will create a secondary chi flow—buffering the stove area from the chi flow.

Be certain the walkway between an island and stove is 40"–48" wide. If not, hang a light above the walkway to energetically expand the area.

Be certain counters are 26"–28" wide. If narrower accidents will increase. If counters are too deep, fill them with plants.

Out of reach is out of balance

To grab for something beyond your reach might be great in business, but constantly needing to stand on tiptoes to get your breakfast cereal or put glasses away can lead you to think that much of life is "beyond your reach." Besides the fact that almost half of kitchen accidents involving children are caused by reaching for something high above their heads; constant reaching is tiring. When people get tired of reaching, they avoid using anything beyond the second shelf. They gradually reduce use of their kitchen to half of the available space. If it's on the top shelf, forget it. Self-imposed limits are dangerous in the kitchen. Because this area symbolizes the ability to generate life-force energy, people who "make do" with half a kitchen, live a "make do" life.

Invest in a step stool. You can get great step stools now that will actually enhance the design of your kitchen, rather than detract from it. A step stool also changes how children interact with the kitchen. When children can reach their own glasses or get their own cereal bowls, their naturally independent and inquisitive natures blossom and expand. They begin to do things on their own that they used to ask mom to do. And they begin to wonder what else they could do, if only they had the tools. Don't be surprised if buying a step stool initiates conversations with your youngster of how to build a rocket ship or program a computer. And don't be surprised if you find yourself using that step stool more than you thought you would.

The edge of this wall projects out into the space, creating a poison arrow. The owner has softened the point by placing a tall plant along the edge.

Prevent poison arrows

Poison arrows refer to any sharp edge or point that directs energy towards you. Three to four times as much energy funnels off a point as comes off a flat wall. Such an intense, penetrating energy is invasive and punctures openings in your energetic field. When you repeatedly walk by a sharp point, your body constantly needs to repair these puncture wounds. Kitchen countertops tend to be a common source of poison arrows. Granite and other hard surfaces, although preferred for other reasons, create jagged penetrating energy if the corners are not rounded.

Poison arrows

Be aware of poison arrows such as:

- refrigerators and cupboards that jut out

- islands with jagged edges

- shelves with sharp corners

Simply moving the microwave over a bit and placing a plant in between the refrigerator and the microwave will reduce EMFs.

Be certain the refrigerator, microwave, TV, and other electrically charged objects are further than two feet apart. This reduces compounded EMFs, which can leap farther out into a room.

How to reduce EMFs

To reduce EMFs in your kitchen, increase Wood and decrease Metal. Wood is an insulator; metal is a conductor. Every wood cabinet, wood stirring spoon, or chopping board reduces radiation. Each metal object, including the stove, refrigerator, dishwasher, and faucet increases radiation.

Where the wires are—EMF alert

What's running behind your walls is as important in feng shui as what you hang on them. An average kitchen has numerous forms of radiation. Microwaves, refrigerators, cell phones, TVs, and kitchen radios all serve to cut us off from the earth's natural resonance. We lose the ability to hear our own bodies' electromagnetic messages and tend to feel out of balance, irritable, and dizzy. The body's need to stabilize these drastically different radiations also places considerable strain on the immune system and creates fatigue. Overall, prolonged exposure to high radiation is a major cause of depression in adults and hyperactivity in children. When you subject yourself to man-made high electromagnetic fields, you greatly reduce your body's ability to generate and sustain life.

The bad news—electricity jumps. In fact, wires in a transformer box don't even physically touch; they induct electricity. That is, the wires are coiled close to each other and the electricity jumps from one to the other.

The good news—you don't have to be very far away from EMFs in order to be out of harm's way. Normal household EMFs reduce drastically within a foot or two, so placement plays a key role in reducing the stress on the body caused by these radiations. Position light switches and electrical plug-ins away from sitting and eating areas. Always unplug your toaster after using it.

Why painters can't get health insurance

Painters have a hard time getting health insurance because insurance companies know something you might not. Paint is extremely toxic, especially while it's drying. We have made great progress in creating low-VOC paints (VOC stands for Volatile Organic Compounds) if you know to ask for them. Major paint companies now carry low-VOC lines. (Beware companies with paint lines titled "Low-odor." Often this means that they have added a perfuming agent to the same toxic paint to cover up the smell.) Even when you use a low-VOC paint, leave the windows open and avoid using the room for 2–3 days afterwards.

Natural paints—contain no preservatives or fungicides. Pigments are derived from clay, minerals, and plants. The solvents used are lemon and citrus oils. These paints often have a strong citrus odor.

Milk paint—made from milk products and various minerals. It comes in powder form and you add the water, which eliminates the need for solvents to keep it in liquid form. Makes a great antique finish on walls and wood, but doesn't stand up well to wear.

Low-biocide paints—conventional water-based paints with the omission of 95% of the preservatives and fungicides. Because of the lack of fungicides, don't use them in bathrooms or other humid areas. Because of the lack of pesticides, don't use paint that has been stored for over six months.

Where are your cleaning supplies?

Avoid storing cleaners, mops, brooms, and vacuum cleaners in the same cupboard as your food. Plan for a utility sink where mops can be washed out and paintbrushes cleaned, that's not in your cooking area.

Cleaning items deserve their own cupboard—far away from the food.

Dangers of heating systems

Your heating system could be one of your biggest health problems, especially if it's located close to the kitchen.

Carbon dioxide, carbon monoxide, and hydrocarbons are all released from your central heating system on a daily basis. If these fumes are allowed to build up in the home, you could experience:

- **fatigue**

- **depression**

- **respiratory problems**

- **headaches**

- **dizziness**

- **nausea**

- **flu-like symptoms**

Keep the kitchen as far away from the central heating system as possble.

Why forced air doesn't work

Our skin is designed to keep forceful elements out of our bodies, and that includes forced air from heating systems. The skin actually closes its pores as a protective mechanism. Human beings heat up fastest, not through the skin, but through the bone and muscle density, hence the saying, "cold to the bone." Radiant heat, the way the sun heats the earth, is the most effective natural form of heating a home and thereby heating our bodies. The heat from a fire, bricks in the bottom of the bed, a hot bath, are all forms of radiant heat. They naturally feel good and warm you faster than sitting next to a heater vent. Forced air is, by nature, inconstant and your body has to work harder to stabilize.

Cold winter mornings are best spent in a kitchen with a radiant heat source. If winters last more than a month or two in your neighborhood, consider adding a corner kiva or wood-burning stove in your kitchen. These areas are kid magnets, drawing children out of chilly bedrooms into the heart of the home. Better than a flu shot, radiant heat in the morning can reduce the amount of colds and sickness your children suffer during a normal winter by raising their body temperature and, thereby, increasing their resistance to viruses and infections. The less energy they use keeping warm, the more able they are to fight off disease.

What's ionization doing in my kitchen?

The molecules that make up all living things have a nucleus with orbiting electrons. The nucleus is made up of protons, which have a positive electric charge. The orbiting electrons have a negative electric charge. These electrons are small and light and they can easily get bumped out of their orbit, usually by static, friction, or pollution. This disrupts the positive/negative balance of the molecule, and instead of being "neutral," the molecule is now positively charged. This positive charge is called a positive ion. Positive ions are present in polluted, stagnant air.

When the positive ion count jumps, you might find yourself feeling unusually sleepy, hard to get motivated, or depressed. If you take steps to shift the ionization balance in your home, you can expect to reduce hay fever and asthma, SAD (Seasonal Affective Disorder), and seritonin imbalances, which lead to lethargy and fatigue.

Architect Dale Bates, of _Living Architecture_, enhances ionization by leaving the foundation open to the earth at some place in the home and by pouring water over rocks that are in contact with the earth's surface. These areas make natural year-round planter boxes. Running water over natural earth and rock creates a strong negative ionic balance.

Generating negative ions

There are numerous ways to generate more negative ions into your kitchen and bring the electric charge back into balance.

- **If remodeling, add a fireplace or kitchen kiva.**

- **Make certain cooking and heating fumes are properly ventilated.**

- **Opt for evaporative coolers over air conditioning.**

- **Incorporate dust-free surfaces and dust often.**

- **Replace synthetic building materials with natural stone, wood, etc.**

- **Replace plastic containers with ceramic pots.**

- **Consider an ionizer.**

How healthy is your kitchen?

The following quiz will expand your awareness of how your home's construction affects your health.

What's on your walls?

Water-based paints—emit toxic chemicals and preservatives for up to six months.

Oil-based paints—give off large amounts of volatile gases as they dry and cure, and react with ultra-violet light to produce ozone.

Paneling—is made from pressed particleboard which contains large amounts of formaldehyde.

Vinyl wallpapers—are covered with vinyl plastic, which emit vinyl chloride.

Conventional wallpapers—are dyed with chemical inks and treated with mildecides, fire retardants, and stain guards.

What's on your floors?

Hardwood floors—are comprised of resin and solvent, which emit toxins during application and drying time for up to six months.

Synthetic carpets—harbor dust and house mites in the backing. When installed, up to 40 different chemicals are emitted from the adhesive backing for at least three days.

Vinyl—emits toxins for the first 24 hours after installation.

Stain protectors—contain insecticides, fungicides, fire retardants, and stain repellents.

Unglazed ceramic tiles—harbor bacteria and microorganisms.

How clean is your water?

Tap water—can contain chlorine, fluoride, lead, and other metals.

Bottled water—is often transported in tankers that also carry fuels and liquid gases. Plastic water bottles emit plastic chemicals within as little as 24 hours.

How clean is your air?

Air conditioning—is the number one cause of asthma inflammators. Coolants contain chemicals, which can constrict the lungs and generate positive ions.

Conventional filters—need to be changed once a week to effectively remove particles.

Countertops?

Granite—needs a periodic application of a protective sealant to ward off stains.

Marble—is much softer than granite and needs frequent applications of sealant.

Engineered quartz—needs no sealant because of the resin binders which makes it nonporous.

Ceramic tile—grout areas allow mold and bacteria to grow, requiring regular cleaning.

Concrete—requires mineral oil or paste wax to keep surface smooth and color uniform, no unnatural sealants are needed.

Wood—can be sealed with mineral oil. Avoid cutting on the wood or mold grows in the cuts.

Stainless steel—is maintenance free and about as healthy as it gets.

For interior walls with no outdoor view, bring the healing energy of nature into your kitchen through plants and artwork.

Can your kitchen breathe?

If you're remodeling, or just want to know how healthy your kitchen is, consider the effect of high-powered ranges on the quality of your air. It is great to have a professional range, but be certain the range hood is strong enough to adequately vent the higher heat output. If you have a high-quality range hood that blows it out, you also need to guard against negative air pressure. Whenever negative air pressure occurs, air tries to enter your home wherever it can—including through furnaces and fireplaces. This can bring combustion by-products, such as carbon monoxide back inside your home. To prevent this, be certain you have either walls that breathe, such as a block wall, or vent fresh air into the kitchen with fans that blow air into the home, or by ducts leading from outside into the kitchen.

To break up stagnant chi, walk through the kitchen shaking a rattle such as the one above, or ringing a chime.

Dishwashing
& nirvana —spirituality of chores

One of the most frustrating aspects of home life is that some things need to be done over and over again. Dishwashing, sweeping, wiping down counters, all for a few moments of cleanliness. It's easy to feel that these efforts are in vain. But a key feng shui teaching is that every "mundane" action has an effect in the transcendental or "transpersonal" realm. Your cleaning has as much to do with your soul's desire to experience a certain physical reality as it does with your ego's satisfaction in a clean house. And your ego might not get as frustrated with the seemingly mundane nature of your tasks if you understand some of their transcendental meanings.

above: Placing a symbolic object, such as this radiometer, next to your kitchen sink can serve as a reminder that the transcendental and the mundane are inextricably linked.

right: Since washing dishes is something we do daily, why not plan for a stunning view out the sink window. It can help transform a dirty task into a meditative act.

Lemons have the ability to draw tension out of the body and help you release it.

If you honor yourself with healthy, balanced meals and clean surroundings; you are more likely to have a healthy, balanced, organized home and personal life.

Some of the most mundane chores in the kitchen include washing dishes, cleaning out the refrigerator, sweeping the floor, and clearing off the counters. However, each of these activities brings a rewarding benefit to the home.

Dishwashing gives us the ability to restore an object, such as a plate, to its pristine original condition. Submerging dirty dishes into warm water and withdrawing clean dishes that are ready to be used again, represents the act of baptism. Whether or not you adhere to a Christian faith, the act of baptism is one of renewal. Every time we wash dishes, we perform an act of renewal. Focusing your attention on what it is you'd like to renew, or what type of new beginning you'd like to have, is a great way to transform the act of washing dishes into a spiritual experience.

Cleaning out your refrigerator can be a symbolic gesture for clearing out of your life anything that no longer serves you, is no longer "present time," and has begun to rot. Rot and decay are nature's way of keeping our energy in the present moment. Just as you would not eat something past its stage of ripeness, you should also not stay in a job past its appropriate time or continue in a relationship that has begun to decay. Clean out your refrigerator and pay attention to what comes to mind while you do so. Then fill the refrigerator with healthy ripe food, representing your ability to draw to you whatever new energy or situation you desire.

In feng shui, the floor represents your past, your foundation, and that from which you came. Past-time energy is held in floors, which can make it harder to break old patterns and begin a new way of doing things. The act of sweeping clears away the dross and leaves only the refined essence.

Sweeping the floor is a way to remove any energy from the day before and allow each new day to hold its own.

For traumatic events, you'll need to do more than sweep. To clear trauma energy, fill a bucket with warm water and add ⅓ cup of white vinegar. Cut a fresh lemon into nine slices. As you place each slice in the water, visualize that the astringent properties of the lemon have the ability to pull out and remove any lingering emotions or tension from the floor. While mopping, continue to visualize that you are drawing to your mop any lingering strands of energy that might hold you in the past or trigger emotions surrounding the past event. Draw them all into your mop, dump them into the bucket, and wash them down the drain. You can live this new day without them.

Horizontal surfaces such as countertops tend to gather things throughout the day. If you don't clear off your counters at least once a day, you have entered "the piling zone." The piling zone is a place where energy accumulates faster than it is dispersed. Although we want to gather chi, piles are stuck chi that can't move. If things have begun to pile up on your countertops, you've probably felt the effects of this stuck, stagnating chi. Things begin to feel heavier than they were before, you're easily overwhelmed, and your ability to make decisions seems to wane. Dealing with counter clutter can be a simple matter of focus or a huge emotional hurdle.

How much clutter is too much? This is a common question. Some people like to keep all their spices out on the counter so they don't have to dig around for them, others leave nothing out, not even a coffeemaker or toaster. Although there are personality differences here the goal is to have a clear working space so energy can move. Use your own emotions as your gauge.

For a Self-knowledge area in a kitchen, use stoneware pots to increase the association with earth and inner stability.

If you feel unable to hold onto your chi, place a plant or a bowl full of fresh fruit on the counter to slow and hold the energy.

The three secrets

The three secrets are one of Grand Master Lin Yun's most powerful contributions to the practice of feng shui. The three secrets move feng shui beyond the realm of physical shifts in energy to the realm of the transcendental, which shifts on a mental, emotional, and soul level. The mind, emotions, and soul, coupled with the physical body, make a complete person. To alter your situation in a holistic way, integrating the physical, mental, emotional, and spiritual aspects of your being, combine your feng shui cures with the three secrets.

The three secrets use specific techniques to align different aspects of your being with the change you are inviting into your life. To use the three secrets, begin with a well-defined intention. After defining your intention, perform the following three actions.

- **Align your physical body by holding a mudra.**

- **Align your mental self by visualizing the desired change.**

- **Align your soul by speaking a mantra.**

All three of these actions act upon the emotions, creating a shift in that fourth aspect of your being.

Mudras (sacred hand postures)

The mudra is the aspect of the adjustment that symbolically aligns the power of your physical body with the change. Although it uses the hands, it requires that you focus and align your entire body with the energy or vibration that you are calling into your life. There are three specific mudras used in black hat feng shui.

The dispelling mudra. This mudra is used to remove or release energies in your auric field that are not in harmony with your intention. To perform this mudra, fold your middle two fingers under your thumb and then flick them up and out. Perform this motion nine times before performing the other two secrets. Traditionally men performed this action with their left hand while women used the right. I recommend using both hands, as it integrates both yin and yang aspects and makes for a more powerful adjustment.

The heart sutra mudra. This mudra is a posture traditionally held while chanting the heart sutra, a prayer for calming the heart and soul and for transcending the physical realm. For this posture, place your right hand on top of your left (for women) or left hand on top of your right (for men), thumbs barely touching. Hold your hand close to your body, right above your stomach. Imagine that energy is moving with the breath in and out through the circle created by your hands. Now imagine that this stream of energy opens a vortex or energetic transport to another realm. You are able to travel to this other realm through the energetic opening held by your hands. Here you feel completely peaceful and calm. Hold this position while performing the other two secrets. The heart sutra mudra is used to hold in place all the good things that you have already received.

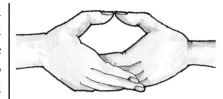

The invitation mudra. While the first two mudras help you let go of what you don't want, and embrace what you already have, the invitation mudra helps you invite in new things. This mudra is performed by curling the two middle fingers under the thumb (as in the dispelling mudra) except that this time you turn your palms up, first and pinky fingers extended. Hold this position while performing the other two secrets.

Visualizations

Bringing your mind into alignment with your desired result is a crucial part of the manifestation process. Your thoughts and mental imagery continuously create your future, telling you what is and isn't possible for you, what things mean, and how you should respond to them. You can choose to interpret events in a way that serves, rather than limits. Your mind enables you to shift your energy from hoping something will happen to acting as if something has already happened. This shift in energy is a tool to activate dormant energy reserves and put them to good use.

Anything you accomplish or become is the result of cooperative energy from those around you. Rather than manipulating or changing others, energetically gift them with what they need in order to interact with you in a mutually beneficial way. When you create this possibility energetically, you increase the chances of it happening on other levels as well.

Mantras

Working with mantras requires two types of action—investment and repetition.

(1) To invest the mantra with your chi, sit quietly and repeat the mantra to yourself for at least 10 minutes, letting the various shades of meaning sink in, until you feel connected to what the mantra is saying to you personally. Journal to keep these meanings conscious.

(2) After having invested your mantra, use an object to remind you to repeat the mantra often throughout the day. Every time you pass the object or think about it, it should automatically bring the mantra to mind. Position the object so that it is in your view where you work through difficult emotions or issues. You might want a mantra object on your desk for when you make difficult phone calls, or by your child's bedside to remind you of your intentions for how you want to relate to the child. Let your repetitions give you the insight and the spaciousness of mind to choose new responses to life events, rather than giving in to old patterns.

Mantras (sacred sounds)

Mantras are sacred sounds which, when uttered, alter surrounding energy patterns. Every sound you make changes the vibration of your environment. Once uttered, sound spreads out, altering everything it encounters, until, slowly, its kinetic energy is transformed into potential energy again. When you utter sounds while holding a mudra and visualizing an intention, you use sound's ability to penetrate and molecularly alter the surrounding environment, bringing that environment into alignment with your goal. The following mantras are often used in performing the three secrets.

Om Ma Ni Pad Me Um. Often called the six words of truth, this is a Buddhist mantra that is literally translated as "the jewel is in the eye of the lotus." It is pronounced ohm mah nee pad may uhm. It bespeaks a recognition that everything originates from the same energetic source, the "tao," and that all beings are varying manifestations of this universal energy flow. It is believed that uttering this mantra will align you and your life with your tao, or life purpose, restoring harmony and balance. Repeat this mantra nine times as part of the three secrets.

Gate Gate. This mantra is an excerpt of the Heart Sutra, a famous Buddhist prayer for letting go of the desires of this world and aligning oneself with universal forces.
Gate, Gate "gāhtay, gāhtay"
(gone, gone)
Para Gate "parah gāhtay"
(gone beyond)
Para Sam Gate "parah sāhm gāhtay"
(gone even further beyond)
Bodhi Svaha "bodhee, sehvah, hah"
(into infinity)
This mantra is traditionally repeated nine times as part of the three secrets.

For each feng shui adjustment that you carry out, be certain to reinforce that adjustment by using the three secrets. It will strengthen your intention and create energetic alignment between your body, your mind, and your soul. The more these different aspects of your being align, the greater your personal power and the stronger your ability to manifest your desires in your life.

Acknowledgments

Anyone who benefits from this book should first thank the many clients who were willing to honestly access their lives, see what was and wasn't working for them, and risk making changes. I am grateful to the following clients, feng shui consultants, and interior designers for sharing their kitchens with me: Lexa Ayer, a prior feng shui student who has evolved into a master consultant; Mary Dennis of Feng Shui 2000, whose top-of-the-line work can be seen in the remodel section; Janet Kaufmann, whose kitchen remodel transformed the entire house; Mimi Amrit, an interior designer who works with energy as much as objects; Polly Reynolds, for getting organized and allowing us to benefit from the process; Jana Whiting, for allowing her clutter-clearing to be photographed and put into print; Kathy Levinson, for creating a home of beauty and balance; Sue White, an interior designer with Betty Rumpf Interiors; Katie Mercier of Eiffel Tower West Catering; and the many others who chose to remain anonymous.

Anyone who benefited from the chapter on organizing and clutter-clearing, please thank Marla Dee of Clear and Simple Solutions for her years of experience and hands-on work with her clients. Many of the healthy homes in this book are the work of Dale Bates (Living Architecture) and Dennis Kavenaugh (Kavenaugh Construction). My thanks to Scot Zimmerman of Zimmerman Photography for making interior photography an art form. As a feng shui consultant, I am also grateful for an editor Laura Best and illustrator Shauna Mooney Kawasaki, who understood that the layout and design of this book was as important as the text and photographs. My thanks also to Jo Packham and the team of helpful, cheerful souls at Chapelle, Ltd., for supporting this project through its many stages.

You should know that my children Ryan and Austin didn't go without dinner while I wrote this book and that my husband Kent thinks I should write a new book every year, because it brings me incredible joy to share myself in this way. It is great to have such a supportive and loving family in my life.

Resources

Feng Shui Practitioner Training Programs
The Feng Shui Training Center
877-470-7769
PO Box 567, Salt Lake City, Utah 84110
www.thefengshuitrainingcenter.com
fstc@xmission.com
Feng Shui Practitioners and Professional Organizers
The best resource for locating a practitioner in your area is The International Feng Shui Guild.

159

About the author

Sharon's interest in the healing power of homes began in 1994 in response to a debilitating and chronic illness.

She studied with numerous teachers, including Carol Bridges and Denise Linn, to gain a broad understanding of a number of approaches to the art of feng shui.

Since then, Sharon has worked with homeowners, designers, architects, and builders to create environments that honor and support the people living in them. Her intention is to help people use their homes to open a communication channel between their external and internal worlds.

She believes the most powerful feng shui adjustments are those that help people change their internal reality and, thereby, dramatically alter their lives. Sharon Stasney is the author of *Feng Shui Chic*, a best-selling introduction using modern applications of ancient feng shui wisdom.

Index